# IRELAND THROUGH TUDOR EYES

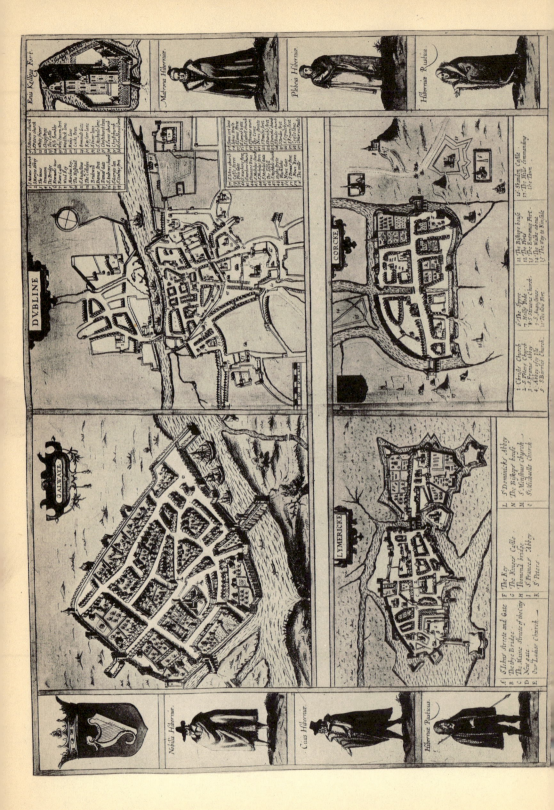

# Ireland

## Through Tudor Eyes

By

EDWARD M. HINTON

PHILADELPHIA: UNIVERSITY OF PENNSYLVANIA PRESS

London: Humphrey Milford: Oxford University Press

1935

*To*

F. E. S.

# Foreword

THE period of Irish history dealt with in this study extends roughly from the death of Shane O'Neill in 1568 to the death of Hugh Roe O'Neill in 1616.

Prior to the crushing of the first O'Neill rebellion Ireland had been in a constant and violent state of unrest. By 1616 the position of English supremacy in Ireland was secure. It was during the interval between these dates that the island was first effectually subdued and the first successful plantations carried out. And it was this period of unrest and opportunity that attracted to Ireland soldiers of fortune of daring and colorful type.

From 1569 to the end of the century a succession of versatile young men sailed for Ireland from England, from France, and from the Low countries. Most of them had been Oxford or Cambridge men, most of them had seen service in the Dutch Wars, most of them were of good English families. They exemplify, like those who have come after them, how closely the history of British Empire is bound up with the biographies of her younger sons.

Many of the names that follow are associated with literary history as pamphleteers and poets. The twofold purpose of this essay is, first to group those writers who through common experience and effort had a part in the subjugation of Ireland for Elizabeth, and, second, to suggest that the writings here dealt with, though touching on social history in the main, are not wholly wanting in literary interest as well.

Concerning the method adopted, a word is perhaps due. Historical data, pursuant to the intent of this study, is based upon the Tudor chroniclers, Campion, Stanihurst, and Hooker, within whose experience the period 1556–1586 falls. For the later period, up to and through the rebellion of Hugh Roe O'Neill and the pacification of Ireland under Mountjoy, Moryson's *Journal* has been followed. Into the historical framework, so derived, have been fitted the literary adventurers with which this study has to do, each in his connection as nearly as may be. Quotations have been used where they have definite illustrative value and are consistent with the general design. Certain notes touching on points of earlier history, law, and society have been epitomized from P. W. Joyce's *Short History of Gaelic Ireland* and *The Social History of Ancient Ireland*. Dates have been checked against R. Bagwell's admirable documentary histories, *Ireland under the Tudors* and *Ireland under the Stuarts,* and against the *Calendars of State Papers for Ireland*.

In conclusion I might point out that, while both Irish and Anglo-Irish writing through the reign of Mary have been adequately dealt with elsewhere, and while modern Anglo-Irish literary relations are conventionally dated from Shirley's connection with the Irish stage, the literary history of the intervening period (1568–1625) is a thing of bits and pieces. It is the feeling that an organized treatment of the scattered writings produced at this time has some value in point of historical continuity and social interest both from the standpoint of Irish letters and English, that prompts the writer in his effort to present *Ireland Through Tudor Eyes.*

E. M. H.

*Philadelphia*
*October 1935*

# Contents

# Illustrations

# I

# *Tudor Ireland*

The land of Ireland is uneven, mountainous, soft, watery, woody, and open to winds and floods of rain, and so fenny, as it hath Bogs upon the very tops of Mountains, not bearing man or beast, but dangerous to pass, and such Bogs are frequent all over Ireland. Our Mariners observe the sailing into Ireland to be more dangerous, not only because many tides meeting, makes the sea apt to swell upon any storm, but especially because they ever find the coast of Ireland covered with mists, whereas the coast of England is commonly clear, and to be seen far off.[1]

**I**RELAND, then, in 1579 was topographically much as it is today, a shallow inland basin, girdled with hilly coasts, moist in climate, rich in lakes and rivers.

Country roads were few, and their winding courses were commanded at fords and at other strategic points by the fortified castles of the old Anglo-Irish families who, after generations in the country, were hardly less predatory than the wild Irish about them.[2] Thieves and marauders were so common that from time to time open bounty was offered on their heads. Merchants habitually traveled in companies for safety, and for an English official to move beyond the Pale without armed escort was to invite disaster. Where possible, communication and travel were by sea.

Owing to a confused and debased coinage which the English government farmed out to private speculators, wealth throughout Ireland was reckoned in land and cattle, and the latter became the principal medium of exchange.

War had become more than ever the principal business of living since the dissolution of the monasteries with their schools in the reign of King Henry VIII. In education it was a far cry to the splendid Irish church foundations of the seventh, eighth, and ninth centuries, whither scholars

[1] Fynes Moryson, *Itinerary*, IV, 191.
[2] G. B. O'Connor, *Elizabethan Ireland*, p. 231.

from England and continental Europe had come, building streets of sod huts in the sanctuary of the monastery grove, and spending their days in the cells of the learned divines.[3] Campion, even so late as 1571, describes the education of the native Irish as being in the hands of the brehons, physicians, and lower clergy.

> Without either precepts or observations of congruity, they speak Latin like a vulgar language, learned in their common Schools of Leachcraft and Law, whereat they begin Children, and hold on sixteen or twenty years conning by rote the Aphorisms of Hypocrates, and the Civil Institutions, and a few other parings of these two faculties. I have seen them where they kept School, ten in some one Chamber, groveling upon couches of straw, their Books at their noses, themselves lying, flat prostrate, and so to chant out their lessons by piecemeal, being the most part lusty fellows of twenty five years and upwards.[4]

In such schools as these the children of the lower tribal chiefs were taught. The higher gentry and nobility, like the merchant and official families of the towns, were in a better position, many sending their sons to the universities of England or the Continent, or giving them traveling tutors.

The houses of the peasant farmers were built as a rule upon hilltops or on artificial mounds. Characteristically, they were circular and hive-shaped, and were made by bedding poles in the earth at short intervals along a circular diameter, weaving wythes and branches in and out between the poles as wicker is woven, and plastering inside and out with mud and lime.[5] Among Irish of the lower classes, livestock might be driven indoors at night to keep it safe from thieves.

The farmsteads of the better-to-do were surrounded by a rampart, planted with thick hedge and having a single entrance, and into this enclosure the cattle were driven. The house, larger perhaps, was on the same plan.

[3] P. W. Joyce, *A Social History of Ancient Ireland*, I, 408 ff.
[4] Edmund Campion, *History of Ireland*, 1571, p. 26.
[5] P. W. Joyce, *A Social History of Ancient Ireland*, 1920. II, 23 ff.

The houses of the intermediate chiefs, sometimes quite large, were of oak after the English fashion, and seem, even so late as Elizabeth's day, to have been protected by circular ramps of earth planted with thorn or hedge. The interior arrangement, like that of the lower orders, however, continued to be a single apartment, a separate chamber being sometimes built and reserved for the women of the household.[6] The use of lake dwellings or crannoges, artificial islands with fortified wooden houses on them, was common. Sir Josias Bodley, who has a later place in this study, solved once and for all the tactical problem of crannoge attack by the use of arrows tipped with wildfire. So much for the more settled elements of the population.

In the time of Queen Elizabeth there were sixty of the Celtic Irish chieftains who lived only by the sword and obeyed no temporal power. Each had a following of seven or eight hundred retainers called *kerne,* who, when not fighting under their chiefs, were engaged in plunder. These wild Irish led a nomad existence, tending cattle and growing a little corn, the latter for their horses.[7] They rarely built houses and were sheltered alike from heat and cold by the Irish cloak. Strife and pillage were the main businesses of their lives.

In the account of the wild Irish written in 1566 by J. Goode, a priest educated at Oxford, afterwards schoolmaster at Limerick, the following description of the kern is given:

They generally go bare-headed save when they wear a head-piece; having a long head of hair, with curled gleebes, which they highly value, and take it hainously if one twitch or pull them. They wear linen shifts, very large, with wide sleeves down to their knees, which they generally dye with saffron. They have woolen jackets, but very short; plain breeches, close to their thighs, and over these they cast their mantles or shag-rugs, which Isadore calls *Heteromallae,* fringed with an agreeable mixture of colors, in which they wrap themselves up, and sleep upon

[6] P. W. Joyce, *A Social History of Ancient Ireland,* 1920. II, 42.
[7] E. Campion, *History of Ireland,* 1571 (Sir J. Ware, ed., 1809), p. 25.

the bare ground. Such also do the women cast over the garment which comes down to their ankles, and they load their heads, rather than adorn them, with several ells of fine linen roll'd up in wreaths, as they do their necks with necklaces, and their arms with bracelets.[8]

On Moryson's authority these shirts were dyed with saffron as a deterrent to vermin, as the Irish seldom put them off till they were worn out. Campion drily mitigates the stricture with the comment that in his time the use of saffron was on the wane, the Irish having learned to wash their linen four and five times in the year.[9]

Stanihurst writes that the food of the wild Irish consisted largely of meat, cresses, roots and herbs, oatmeal and buttermilk, beef broth, and *aqua vitae*. Spenser mentions the fondness of the Irish for black blood pudding, and the custom of bleeding animals for emergency food was common among soldiers in the field.[10] The use of the white potato was reserved for a later age, although Sir Walter Raleigh is credited with having introduced it into Ireland as early as 1573.[11]

It is important to bear in mind that, subsequent to the reign of King Henry VIII, the Old English or Anglo-Irish families dominated Meath, Connaught, Leinster, and Munster; of Ireland's five provinces Ulster alone remained in the hands of the traditional Celtic chiefs, the O'Cahans, the O'Donnels, and the O'Neills. The two branches of the great Geraldine family, the house of Fitzgerald in Munster and of Kildare in Leinster, and the Ormonde Butlers of Munster and Connaught, were lords of the south. Under the walls of their castles clustered the cottages of their immediate retainers, and their respective countries were held by the ramparted farmsteads of their sept chiefs and tenant farmers, among whose duties were those of bearing arms on

---

[8] J. Small (ed.), J. Derricke, *Image of Ireland*, 1581. v. Introduction (1883).
[9] *History of Ireland*, p. 25.
[10] *Ibid.*; E. Spenser, *View of the State of Ireland*, 1596.
[11] *D. N. B.*

the occasion of a muster or rising out, and of maintaining the chief and his professional guard of gallowglasses and horse.

Of soldiers, according to Stanihurst,[12] the horseman was next below the chief or captain. Every horseman was attended by a groom or horseboy who in turn had at his service a lackey, "a little young wag called a Daltin." On the evidence of Hooker,[13] each horseman had at his service not one but several mounts of which the Irish hobby was trained for ordinary hacking, and the running breeds imported from the Spanish peninsula were used only for skirmish and battle. The Irish horseman learned to mount from off side or near—how well, is illustrated in a very human way by Stanihurst's anecdote of Sir Walter Raleigh's guide who, being surprised by the Seneschal of Imokilly at a marshy ford, sprang so high that he overleapt his mount entirely and dove into a bog.[14] Barnabe Rych also testifies to the expertness of Irish horsemen who, riding without saddle or stirrups, clad in leather and armed only with light spears, swords, and targets, never hesitated to meet the mixed bands of English pikes and calivers in headlong charge.[15]

Next below the horseman in degree of honor was the gallowglass or heavy-armed infantryman, who wore helmet and linked corslet of knee length, and fought with sword and axe. The gallowglass was chosen for size and strength, had one attendant, and was, like the horseman, a fighter by profession.

Last and lowest in military degree was the wild kern or common soldier, a name extended by loose English usage to include the Irish tenant farmer subject to military service. The arms borne by the kern up until the reign of Elizabeth consisted of throwing spear or bow and arrow, buckler,

[12] Stanihurst in *Holinshed*, VI, 68.
[13] *Ibid.*, VI, 21.
[14] *Ibid.*, VI, 441.
[15] B. Rych, *A New Description of Ireland*, 1610.

and short sword or *skene*.[16] Essentially the kern was a knifer; proverbially swift of foot, he was said to be able, in the thickly wooded and boggy country that was his fighting ground, to outrun a horse and pull the enemy rider from the saddle. During the latter part of the reign the caliver and musket began to come into use among the Irish,[17] and, by the nineties, even the wild Irish seem to have adopted English tactics to the extent of alternating pike and shot in formation warfare.

In the walled towns of the east coast and those of the coastal rivers, the predominance of English culture in speech, dress, law, and education was absolute.[18] The seat of government lay in the Castle at Dublin which, like every other garrison city, was the hub of an English sphere of influence and of law. As, in the course of the reign, English garrison outposts advanced northward, southward, and westward, and were linked with military communications, Ireland came first under martial, and then English civil law. Crown authority followed the military engineer.

Forty-three walled towns were scattered through Tudor Ireland, all of them dominated by English influence, and all of them built to stand sieges. The greater seaport towns like Cork, Limerick and Galway usually had the quay guarded by a small castle for protection against pirates who were numerous, certain families like the O'Malleys of Clare Island being swashbucklers by profession, and maintaining private navies of from one to three galleys.[19] Maritime towns, therefore, maintained ships both for trade and for protection by sea. The landward sides of such towns were, of course, walled and strongly fortified.[20]

[16] G. B. O'Connor, *Elizabethan Ireland*, p. 215.
[17] Stanihurst in *Holinshed*, VI, 68.
[18] O'Connor, pp. 77–78.
[19] C. O. Mahony, *The Viceroys of Ireland*, 1912, p. 79; Lansdowne MS 144. Ambrose Fourth to Mr. Doctor Caesar: concerning Pirates in several towns in Ireland and praying a commission for the tryal of Pirates to be sent over. Dublin 25 February 1586 (Folium 397).
[20] O'Connor, pp. 80–81.

Streets were narrow and dark, the houses built with thick walls of stone, or of stone and half-timber construction. Dublin, at least, boasted a municipal water supply, fed from an open conduit which the city fathers protected by strict ordinances.[21] Visitations of the plague, however, were frequent.

Both Stanihurst and Camden have left sketchy generalizations concerning the towns, but the best extant account of the greater towns is that reprinted by C. L. Falkiner from the MS of L. Gernon, a citizen and city councilman of Limerick. According to Gernon in his *Discourse of Ireland Anno 1620*, the towns of Ireland worthy to be dignified with the name of city were only eight: Dublin, Waterford, Cork, Limerick, Galway, Kilkenny, Derry and Coleraine:[22]

Dublin (writes Gernon) is the most frequented, more for conveniency than for Maiesty. There reside the deputy, and the Councel; there she receyves intelligences, advertisements, instructions. The buildings are of timber, and of the English forme, and it is resembled to Bristoll, but falleth shorte. The circuit of the Castle is a huge and mighty wall four-square, and of incredible thicknes, built by King John, within it are many fayre buildings, and there the deputy keeps his court. There are two cathedralls under one Archbishopp. St. Patrickes, and Christchurch. St. Patricks is more vast and auncient, the other is in better repayre. The Courtes of Justice (the same as in England) are kept in a large stone building parcell of Christchurch, which is built in forme of a crosse, at the foure ends are the foure courts well adorned, the middle is to walk in. There is a house of Courte where the Judges and other Lawyers have chambers, and a common hall to dyne in, and it is called, the Innes, the Judges, and the Kings Councell make the Benche, in which number I am, the rest are barristers, and atturneys. Further there is a Colledge which is also an University. You will expect to know the state of our state. It is not very magnificent, nor to be disregarded. There is a presence where they stand at all times uncovered, and a clothe of state under which the deputy sitteth. When that he sitteth at meate, there sitt of men of quality as many as the table will contayne. When he goeth abroad in solemne manner, all whom it concernes do attend him.

[21] D. A. Chart, *The Story of Dublin*, 1907, pp. 28–29.
[22] C. L. Falkiner (ed.), *Illustrations of Irish History*, pp. 345 ff.

Before him goe the gentlemen captynes, knights, and officers, all on foote. Then commeth the deputy, ryding in state, and before him a knight bareheaded carrying the sword. After the deputy, the nobles, the Councell, and the Judges, all in footeclothes. His guarde consists of fifty tall men, they weare not redd coates, but soldiers cassockes, and halberts in theyr handes. On principall festivalls, the herauld goes before him in a cote of armes. So much of Dublin.

## Now to Cork:

Cork is a porte of the sea also, but stands in a very bogge and is unhealthy. The building is of stone, and built after the Irish forme, which is Castlewise, and with narrow windows more for strength then for beauty, but they begin to beautify it in better forme. There is the quarry of redd marble, which maketh the towne appeare of a ruddy colour. There is also a cathedral but in decay. It is a populous towne and well compact, but there is nothing in it remarkeable. There is nothing to commend it but the antiquity, and nothinge doth disgrace it so much as theyr obstinacy in the antick religion. Pass on to Limerick.

Lymericke is the place of my commerce, lett me entertayn you with a broad cake and a cupp of sacke as the maner is, you will be the lesse sensible of my tediousnes. Lymericke divides itself into two partes, the high towne, which is compassed with the Shanon, and the base towne, and in forme it doth perforth resemble an hower glasse, being bound together by that bridge which divides the two partes. . . . A philosopher that saw a little towne with a wyde open gate, gave warning to the citizens to shutt up theyr gate, least the towne should runne out. The founders of this citty were more considerate, for they have fensed the base towne with such a huge strong wall that travaylers affirme, they have not seene the like in Europe. It is a mile in compasse, and three men a breast may walke the round. . . . In the highe streete it (the high town) is builte from one gate to the other in one forme, like the Colledges in Oxford, so magnificent that at my first entrance it did amase me, *sed intus cadavera*, noysome & stincking houses. The cathedrall is not large but very lightsome, and by the provydence of the Bishop, fayrely beautifyed within, and as gloriously served with singing and organs. There is in this citty an auncient Castle, the Bishop's pallace, and a stone bridge of fourteen arches. But that which is most notorious to my judgement is the key wall. This wall is extended from the towne walle into the middle of the ryver, and was made for a defence and harbor for the shipping. It is in lengthe about 200 paces, and it is a double wall. In the botome it is a mayne thicknes, and so continueth until it be raysed above high water. Then there is within it a long gallery arched over

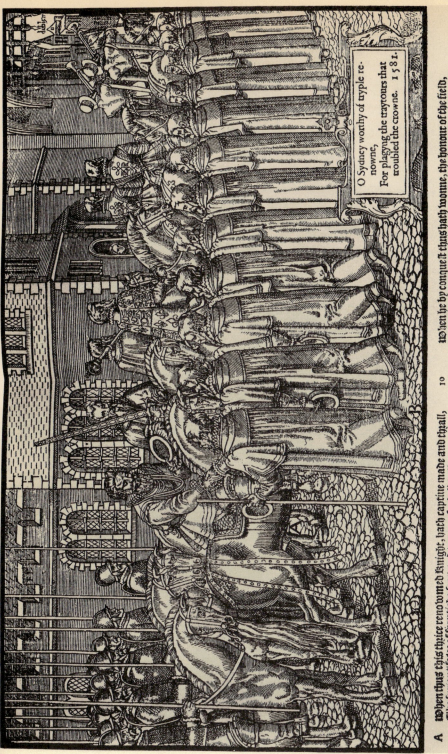

O Sydney worthy of tryple renowne,
For playng the traytours that troubled the crowne.  1581.

A When thus this thrice renowmed knight, hath captiue made and thrall,
The furious force of frantricke foes, and troupe of rebells all,
When he by marshall feates of armes, hath nobly them subdude,
To Princes Dome: whose heauy wrath, their treasons haue renewde,
When he their glory and their pride, hath trampled in the dust,
And brought to naught which doe purdue, the bloudy rebells lust:

When he by conquest thus hath wonne, the honour of the field, 10
And fame vnto our Soueraygnes Coure, report thereof both yeld
And to conclude when honor braue, his trauells to requight
Hath cloth'de him with eternall fame, meete for so great a knight
When all these thinges are done and past, then doth he backe reuart
To Dublyn: where he is received, with ioy on euery parte.

head, and with windowes, most pleasant to walke in, and above that
a tarace to walke upon with fayre battlements, at the end of it there
is a round tower with two or three chambers, one above the other, and
a battlement above. This towne now reioyceth in the residence of the
president. The presidency is kept in the forme as it is in Wales. A president, two Justices and a Councell. We sitt in councell at a table. When
the president goeth forthe, he is attended in military forme, when he
rydeth with a troop of horse, when he walketh with a company of foote
with pikes and musketts in hand. I have kept you too long at Lymerick,
lett me conduct you towards Galloway.

I was never there myself, but it is reported to be the Windsore of
Ireland. It hath been praysed for the magnificent building and a stately
Abbey there, used for a parish churche. But a great fyer which hapned
in May was twelvemonth did consume 400 houses, and utterly defaced
the Abbey being so vehement that the bodyes of the dead lying in the
vaults were consumed to ashes. They beginne to rectify. Let us returne
by Kilkenny.

Of Kilkenny, Waterford, Coleraine and Derry Gernon
writes more briefly. Kilkenny is an inland town pleasantly
situated upon a fresh river and noted for its delightful
orchards and gardens. Waterford is Ireland's best harbor,
English in architecture and famous for merchandise. The
most striking feature of the town is its fortified quay half
a mile in length where ships of a thousand tons burden may
ride at anchor. Coleraine and Derry are of the new plantation; "like new palaces they are not slated, nor the flowers
laid yet. Let them alone till they be finished." Finally, we
have a clear-cut integration of the Irish scene as viewed
by the general traveler:

In this peregrination you have viewed the country in passing, the
villages are distant each from other about two miles. In every village
is a castle, and a church, but both in ruyne. The baser cottages are built
of underwood, called wattle, and covered some with thatch and some
with green sedge, of a round forme and without chimneys, and to my
imaginacion resemble so many hives of bees, about a country farme.

A point that cannot be too strongly stressed is the sharp
social and racial distinction that lay between the English
populations of the towns and the wild Anglo-Irish of the

country. To the town the country kern was "meer" Irish who had no rights at English law. His death, even in time of peace, might be composed for as little as a half-crown. The Irish in many cities were restricted to a quarter outside the walls called "Irishtown," which closely corresponded to the "Darktown" of our own cities. To the country Irishman, contrarily, the townsmen were collectively "Saxon churls" against whose strength and advantage in law his sole redress was force of arms. This social and racial opposition existed until the passage of the antirecusancy laws of Elizabeth's reign drew into common sympathy devout Catholics throughout the island.[23]

Naturally, open dislike of this kind led to fighting. Within sight of Dublin lay the Wicklow hills, the country of the O'Tooles and the O'Byrnes, and Dublin, until quite late in the century, suffered from sudden and savage raids.[24]

A result of the constant battle between town and country was the development of a self-reliant and pugnacious citizenry, administered by bluff mayors and sheriffs, as ready in war as in politics and trade. As a rule, the Lord Deputy and his subordinates, the Lords President of provinces, let the towns alone, seldom undertaking to protect them against raiders on land or pirates by sea.[25] The citizens stood to their own defense, ready to answer the musters, and maintaining small municipal navies. Limerick, noted for its alacrity in supplying musters for Crown campaigns, maintained such a navy, together with a well-armed reserve of a thousand men ready at call, and in Dublin there was a general muster every three months.[26] Little wars between cities were common, and further complicated the picture of Ireland's four hundred septs, constantly at odds in one place or another.

[23] O'Connor, p. 79.
[24] Ibid.
[25] Ibid., p. 87.
[26] Ibid., pp. 88–89.

In other respects the life, dress, and amusements of the
towns did not differ greatly from those of London, which
was at that time, like Dublin, a medieval walled city. For
the populace there was bull and bear baiting, and cockfighting; for the gentry, hawking and hunting, both of
wolf and deer. Dublin had its printers of political and po-
lemical pamphlets, forerunners of the later press, and, like
that, largely the instrument of the Anglican Church.[27]
Miracle and Morality plays seem to have been acted during
the fourteenth century at College Green, Dublin,[28] and
there are hints, here and there, to suggest the existence of
players in Ireland during the reign of Elizabeth who performed secular drama in church properties.[29] Though not
until the days of Shirley did anything like an Irish stage
come into existence, it would have been strange if some of
the London players on tour had not thought to exploit the
ennui incident to garrison life in Ireland.

As one might suppose, writing had a very minor place in
war-ravaged Ireland of the Elizabethan age. Writers of literary history have tended to gloze over as barren ground
the period from the Anglo-Norman invasion to the Rebellion of 1641. But Stanihurst, in his catalogue of Irish
writers, offers a very fair list of native writers of Gaelic,
with a sprinkling of bilinguists and sonneteers.[30] The
weight of opinion is, however, that most of the poetry
made in this era was the work of minstrels, attached after
the ancient and medieval manner to the courts and camps
of the Irish leaders. These "makers" were honored for their
gift of praise, and feared for their ironic commendation of
soldiers who lagged behind the bagpipe.[31]

In the course of the English occupation of turbulent
Ireland, from the Anglo-Norman invasion in the reign of

[27] R. A. Peddie, *Printing, A Short History of the Art*, London, 1927.
[28] Chart, p. 201.
[29] Bagwell, III, 211–212.
[30] Stanihurst in *Holinshed*, VI, 57.
[31] O'Connor, pp. 69–70.

Henry II to the Flight of the Earls of Tyrone and Tyrconnell in 1607, two constant tendencies may be traced: the seizure of land by force of arms, and the attempt by statutory decree to substitute English law for tribal or brehon law, the native Irish system based upon chiefship by election and composition by fine. The bitterness and rebellion that this policy bred, and its consequent three centuries of raid and reprisal, massacre and famine, find close parallels in the bloody chronicle of the Spanish conquest of Mexico.

Owing to the fact that the early English kings were closely occupied with civil and continental wars, no systematic attempt at the absolute subjugation of Ireland was embarked upon until the latter years of King Henry VIII, when the hostile forces of Catholic Italy and Spain began to foster disaffection in Ireland through the influence of the Roman Catholic clergy. The history of English administration in Ireland thereafter is the story of how the successive viceroys extended English garrison towns into the great Irish and Anglo-Irish seignories, forming shire after shire, their extension of Crown authority being bitterly contested by the Irish at every step. The Earl of Sussex, viceroy in the reign of King Edward VI, succeeded in establishing two counties, Kings and Queens. His successors, Sir Anthony St. Leger and Sir Henry Sidney, continued his policy by frequent armed progresses through the country, and the merciless administration of martial law. But the soldiers at their disposal were too few in number to maintain the numerous fixed garrisons needed for the subjugation of a country where roads were so bad and communication so difficult.

It was not until the second deputyship of Sidney that the Irish question became really crucial in English affairs. Three great rebellions occurred in Elizabeth's reign: the rebellion of Shane O'Neill, the Desmond rebellion with its consequent plantation of Munster, and the rebellion of Hugh Roe O'Neill, Earl of Tyrone. At the root of all three lay Irish opposition to the shiring of their lands, with its attendant evils of partisan Courts of Assize and English gibbets. But more vital, from Elizabeth's point of view, was the fact that all three had been fostered and, in a measure, supported by Jesuit missions and Spanish gold. Moryson, the historian, records that Philip planned at one time to land ten thousand men in Ireland as a base for the invasion of England. Likewise of southern instigation were the plots against Elizabeth that centered round Mary Queen of Scots. To combat the papal emissaries of discord, strict laws were put in force, and the Act of Uniformity and Oath of Supremacy enjoined upon all holders of government offices; in Ireland attendance at the Reformed Church was made compulsory in all cities under actual English jurisdiction. Thus, to social and racial oppositeness, political and, finally, religious animosities came to be joined. To the insular Celt, the word "Anglican" became a symbol of slaughter and spoliation; to the English, "Catholicism" and "treason" were absolute synonyms. Hence, except for the few miles immediately about Dublin, the Ireland of Elizabeth's reign was an armed camp of sullen hate and smoldering rebellion, checked only by the blood-and-iron policy that the viceroys pursued to make effective the handful of soldiers maintained for the Irish service.

We have sketched in outline the general character of Tudor Irish life, and touched upon the basic origins of Irish hatred for their English lords. It is now the place to consider a selected group of English writers and adventurers who came to Ireland during the Desmond wars, Munster plantation, and the O'Neill Rebellion (1567 to 1603), and to indicate against the larger historic background with what aspects of the Irish scene their work and interests are identified.

# II

## Sir Henry Sidney

## and

## Shane O'Neill of Tyrone

### 1558–1567

**I**N 1564 Sir Henry Sidney, soldier, courtier, diplomatist, scholar and—not his least glory—father to Sir Philip, was appointed Lord Deputy of Ireland and, fortified alike by powerful court connections and the successful putting down of the rebellion of Shane O'Neill, held a place in Irish rule for fourteen years. In consequence of this prominence, Sidney is one of the pivot figures for this study; it was in his deputyship that both the O'Neill and the Desmond rebellions took place, with the vast land forfeitures that followed. The Lord Deputy was not merely the Queen's representative in Ireland. To him fell the duty of administering the royal service there, and one of those duties was the appointment of a fit and loyal colonial civil service. Then, as now, it was from the younger sons of England's governing classes that this service was recruited, and, among others, the Lord Deputy found place for many a literary protégé, among them, not unnaturally, some sponsored by his brother-in-law, the Earl of Leicester.

The knowledge of Sidney's support of James Stanihurst in the latter's attempt to restore Dublin University in 1569, for example, attracted to Ireland Edmund Campion, historian and theologian. It was Sidney who allowed and supported the slender title of Sir Peter Carew to vast tracts of land in Munster, Leinster and Connaught, a strong contributing cause of the first Desmond rebellion. It was

Sidney who convened the Irish Parliament of 1569 which attainted Shane O'Neill, extinguished his name, and declared Ulster forfeit to the Queen, an act which led three years later to the tragic attempt by Walter Devereux, first Earl of Essex, in company with Lord Rich and Sir Peter Carew, to subdue and colonize Ulster as a private speculation.

To Sidney influence or to Sidney sponsored enterprise, therefore, may be traced the Irish experience of our first two groups of writers. Of these the earlier group, drawn to Ireland through interests in Munster, comprised John Hooker, historian and translator, and his fellow contributors to *Holinshed's Chronicles*, Edmund Campion and Richard Stanihurst. The second group, crossing to Ulster four years later (1573) with the first Earl Essex, included Barnabe Rych, Barnabe Googe and Thomas Churchyard.

Let us now consider briefly the historical events which created opportunity in Ireland for these venturesome younger sons, and, as an essential prelude to a clear understanding of those events, let us go back a little in point of time and outline the first great Irish rebellion of Elizabeth's reign, the rebellion of Shane O'Neill of Tyrone. With this rebellion begins that period of bitter Irish war which in its chronology closely coincides with the Elizabethan Age and which was to end with the effective extension of English authority and English law to include the entire Kingdom of Ireland. Though prior in date to the strict limits of our study, a short treatment of it is a necessary prelude to any understanding of the subsequent abortive attempt on the part of Walter Devereux, first Earl of Essex to pacify and colonize Ulster in 1573. It presents to us, besides, so clear an illustration of the causes and progress of Irish rebellion in general, that it may in a measure be taken as typical of the two rebellions that followed it.

We have first the three commonest causes of Irish war— rival claimants to a single seignory, two conflicting systems of law as applied to land tenure simultaneously in force, and bitter religious animosity. An overt action touches off the spark; an English force crushes opposition in a short and savage campaign; the lands of the rebellious chief are attainted, declared forfeit to the Crown, and leased cheaply to English speculators whose efforts to plant English settlers on them goad their dispossessed Irish tenants into resorting once again to fire and sword. Thus the vicious circle is closed, one rebellion in its progress laying the train for the next.

Shane O'Neill, son of the Con O'Neill created Earl of Tyrone by Henry VIII, who had sought by the distribution of hereditary titles to stamp out the ancient brehon custom of chiefship by election, had been dispossessed in the title by his father in favor of an elder, but illegitimate brother, Matthew. In time Shane killed Matthew (1558), but Matthew left two sons, Brian and Hugh Roe, to whom the title still descended by English law. Now in 1561 Brian, the elder son, was murdered by Tirlogh Luineach O'Neill, Shane's right-hand man. Brian's brother, Hugh Roe O'Neill, was at that time too young to oppose the power of his uncle, so that Shane, who had long since got himself elected "The" O'Neill by brehon law, was able to plead his own case before Queen Elizabeth with such success that in 1562 she conceded him a degree of official sanction in his captaincy of Tyrone, though the young Hugh Roe remained titular Earl. But this was not enough. Himself scorning an English title with its implied subserviency to the Crown, Shane repudiated the Anglican Church and undertook to restore the integrity of the ancient Celtic kingdom of O'Neill in Ulster. Neighboring chiefs and English administrators alike took alarm, and in 1566 Sir Henry Sidney, then Lord Deputy of Ireland, marched against him and after a year of fighting, drove Shane into the camp of enemy Scots MacDonnells of Antrim who soon killed him.

Tirlogh Luineach, Shane's successor as chief of the O'Neills, made formal submission to Sidney in 1567, but the surface quiet that followed did nothing to remove the danger inherent in the situation of two rival claimants to the headship of Tyrone: Tirlogh Luineach by the election of his clansmen and Hugh Roe O'Neill by the English law of succession. It was the conflict of the two cultures, English and Irish, resulting from this situation that led to repeated attempts on the part of the Queen to pacify Ulster by private grants to English colonists. Let us now, having indicated background, leave in this place the uncertain trend of events in the North, and defer resuming its thread till the year 1573 at which time it bears a closer relation to this study. For now in the South a campaign had begun, the immediate effect of which was to attract to Ireland our earliest group of literary adventurers.

# III

# *The Desmond Rebellion*
# *First Stage*

## 1567-1573

**I**N 1567, not long after Tirlogh Luineach's submission in Ulster, fighting had begun in the southern and western province of Munster between two great Anglo-Irish houses, the Earl of Desmond surnamed Fitzgerald and the Earl of Ormonde surnamed Butler. These houses were traditionally rivals and enemies; the beginning of their quarrel dated from the Wars of the Roses when the Desmonds had followed the White Rose and the Ormondes had followed the Red. The root of their difference at the period with which our study deals lay in the circumstance that the Ormonde Butlers professed loyalty to their English administrators, while the Desmond Geraldines were staunch adherents to the Church of Rome and defenders of the Celtic tradition of their adopted land. The spark that fired the feud was the renewed activity by the English government on the accession of Elizabeth toward the establishment of the Anglican Church in Ireland. James Butler, tenth Earl of Ormonde, declared in favor of it; Gerald Fitzgerald, fifteenth Earl of Desmond, stood fast with Catholic Ireland. Lesser leaders took sides and the peace of Munster dissolved into general fighting.

Sir Henry Sidney marched south and took the Earl Gerald into custody, sending him to England as hostage for the peace of Munster. James Fitzmaurice Fitzgerald, a cousin, now formed a league (1568) to maintain the rights of the Earl Gerald and defend the Roman Catholic faith. Sidney crushed the league, and succeeded in imposing upon the Kingdom a short-lived peace in outward

When flickering fame had fild the eares of marshall men of might,
With rare report of Sydneys praise, (that honorable knight)
And though the bruit in Freshe topic did so ill consume the same,
As who could say in Englands staine, of Iustice there became,
And to maynetayne the sacred right, of such a Vertuue Queene,
For seeking of her Subiectes breath, whose like hath never been,
The great Oneale, to strike, the stroke, in stealing vp the same,

12

And to preserue this noble knight, a way to greater fame,
Amazed with such strawning reportes, and of his owne accord,
Came in prostrating him before, the presence of this Lord,
With humble sute for Princes grace, and mercy to obtayne,
With like request vpon the same, that frendly to attayne,
Who promisde then by pledge of life, and vertue of his hand,
For euer to her noble grace, a subiect true to stand,

And to beseeh in each respect, her honor and her name,
Against all those that durst deface, the glory of the same.
Whenas thing so forth other actions moe, redound vnto the same
Of good Syr Henry Sydney knight, so called by his name.
Lo robert besites in honors fear, most comely to behold,
As two by to reputance, the person of a Queene.

FINIS.

show, but in outward show only. The enforcement of the
Oath of Supremacy and the Act of Uniformity had begun
to alienate from allegiance to the Crown English Catholics
as well as Irish. Religious bitterness grew, owing to the
work of Jesuit missions from Italy and Spain and to the
tales of fugitives who crossed from England to Ireland in
the hope of finding the antirecusancy laws less rigidly
enforceable there. Had further friction been needed to fire
rebellion in Munster, it was soon forthcoming in the pre-
tensions of Sir Peter Carew, a lackland knight, who crossed
to Ireland in 1568, after having sent before him as his legal
agent the historian John Hooker with instructions to investigate an ancient title to lands widely scattered through
Leinster, Meath and Munster, and held by prescription
for centuries by clans of both Butler and Fitzgerald.[1] The
preëmption of title to such lands on the part of Carew
and his like, affirmed with the support of the Lord Deputy
and enforced at the point of English pikes, proved to be
the final aggravation. In 1569 the houses of Desmond and
Ormonde united (1569–1570) for the first time in two
centuries for what was to be the opening curtain of a
general rebellion that dragged on intermittently for ten
years, and ended only with the extinction of the Munster
house of Geraldine and the attainder of all the Desmond
lands. Let us here consider in more detail the quality of
that Sir Peter Carew whose career affords the classic example of the estate-hunting English soldier-of-fortune in
Ireland. A delightful account of Sir Peter's colorful life,
and a naïvely partisan account of the knight's experience
in Ireland—and incidentally of his own—is given by
Hooker in the *Life of Sir Peter Carew*.

[1] Bagwell, II, 139–145.

## JOHN HOOKER

### 1526?–1601

The main points of Hooker's experience as an attorney are those related to his investigation of the titles of Carew, and appear in their best connection with Sir Peter's Irish career. That career, illustrating as it does the partisan interpretation of English law with reckless disregard for the tribal rights of Irish occupants, deserves a more than passing treatment:

> At leisure in Devon Sir Peter thought himself of such lands as persuaded he should have in Ireland, and having evidence of the same which being old and he unlearned was referred to Hooker as a man greatly given to seek and search old records and ancient writings . . . and that he was best able of any in the city of Excester to do him pleasure in this behalf.[2]

Sir Peter sought out Hooker, who satisfied him of his title and advised him to enter claim before the Queen's council, which promptly approved it. Sir Peter then sent Hooker over as legal agent (May 1567). Hooker arrived at Waterford, and proceeded toward Dublin, passing through the country of Odrone, "which was a barony and parcel of the inheritance of the said Sir Peter's, and sundry of whose ancestors had been barons of the same." [3]

In Dublin, Hooker tells us, he found evidence to justify the Carew title to lands not only in Leinster (Odrone country), but in Munster and in Meath. No attainders, statutes of absences, or any alienations or discontinuances were found. Accordingly Sir Peter crossed to Ireland in early August of 1568. Landing at Waterford, he sent for Hooker. While at Waterford he was visited by Thomas Stukeley, at that time Constable in Leighlin and Seneschal of Wexford, and by the chiefs of the Kavanaghs. Sir Peter

[2] J. Hooker, *The Life of Sir Peter Carew* (Archeologica, London, 1840, v. 28).
[3] Hooker, *Life of Sir Peter Carew.*

announced to them all that he had come among them to reclaim his lands.

The Kavanaghs attempted to recover by law, but Sir Peter won his case and was installed as Lord of the Barony of Odrone. Shortly thereafter, Thomas Stukeley, whose sympathies were Roman Catholic, was relieved of his post as Constable of Leighlin and Sir Peter was appointed in his place by a warrant from Sidney dated 27 February 1569. Immediately his dispossessed "tenants" and neighbors began to plot:

> Sundry such conspiracies had been and daily were contrived against him, and for no other cause but because he did not only abolish in his own country, but also inveighed against the wicked and detestable uses of the Irishry in *coyne and livery*, in cosheries and cesses, and such other Irish customs, the same being but the spoiling of the honest subjects and true laborers, and the maintenance of thieves, murderers and the maintenance of all loose and disordered people.

His chief enemy seems to have been Sir Edmond Butler, brother to the Earl of Ormonde, part of whose lands Sir Peter had managed to get. Equally discriminated against and equally unable to obtain legal redress, the Ormonde Butlers joined the Geraldine Desmonds against the English. An English force sent by the Lord Deputy and led by Humphrey Gilbert and Nicholas Maltby made short work of the rebellion. Sir Edmond Butler was besieged both at home and at Kilkenny, and was finally made to submit. Hooker now effects a rapid traverse of two years:

> The year next following (1573) the Earl of Essex having a gift of her Highness of the province of Ulster and a commission for the recovery thereof, went over to Ireland with a great retinue, and Sir Peter Carew being one of his consorts, passed over with him, where, when he had remained awhile and considered the continual troubles, the daily encountering with the enemies, the excessive expenses and the doubtful events, and for a soil of land, though fertile of itself, yet a savage, wild and desolate country, and invironed with deadly enemies, did think then of his own estate . . . and took his journey to Leighlin, and sent letters of earnest request into England to the writer hereof.

So Hooker crossed again to Ireland, traveled to Cork, as advance agent for Carew, "and procured that the Lord Courcy, the Lord Barry Og, MacArty Reighe, the Mac-Swineys, the Mahones, the Odalys, the Odryscolls and others submitted themselves and lands, receiving back the lands as tenants. Likewise the territories of MacArty More, the Earl of Desmond, Lord Fitzmorrys, the Seneschal of Imokilly, Lord Barry of Barrymore, Sir Gorman Mac-Tige"—all of them pretending great joy that Sir Peter would come and live among them.

While Hooker, acting on his principal's instructions, prepared houses at Cork and at Kildare, Sir Peter died (27 November 1575). Hooker then returned to England and does not again appear in Irish affairs.

With Carew came the heyday of the English soldier of fortune in Ireland, and the Anglo-Irish and native Irish alike began to feel, not without reason, that their most ancient rights of possession were no longer safe. Unhappily for the peace of Ireland, the case of Sir Peter Carew was only too typical of many another to follow.

Hooker's other writings pertinent to the present study are his later Irish annals for Holinshed, and his translation of Sylvester Giraldus Cambrensis' Latin history of the Anglo-Norman conquest. Something more of these will be said in our following discussion of his fellow contributors to *Holinshed's Chronicles,* Edmund Campion and Richard Stanihurst.

In 1579, when Carew and Hooker were most active in pressing their fantastic claims, a proposal had come up for the reëstablishment of the ancient University of Dublin under Anglican auspices. Sponsors for the idea were Sir Henry Sidney and James Stanihurst, Recorder of Dublin and Speaker of the Irish House of Commons. The opportunity for preferment in the University, suggested to him perhaps by James Stanihurst's son Richard, then a commoner of University College, Oxford, attracted to Ireland

Edmund Campion, fellow of St. Johns, Oxford, and sometime protégé of Leicester and the Queen.[4]

## EDMUND CAMPION
### 1540–1581

Edmund Campion had achieved court patronage purely
on the merit of his early promise and precocious gifts of
oratory. A Roman Catholic at heart, his ambition led him
for a time to conform to the requirements of the Anglican
Church. But orthodox Catholic belief became more and
more subject to obloquy and persecution, and his enemies
increasingly used his known sympathies as a lever to en-
danger his position at Oxford. In 1569, therefore, he
crossed to Ireland with his friend and pupil, Richard Stanihurst, and continued in Dublin as guest of the latter for
the better part of a year.

Campion had hoped to obtain preferment in the new
University, but the entire project fell flat owing to the
opposition of Anglican prelates. These had no wish to see
such an institution founded by Sidney or Stanihurst, both
of whom were tolerant of Catholics, or entrusted to Campion, who was suspected in Ireland as in England of having Catholic sympathies. He was saved from arrest only
through the protection of Sidney, who promised James
Stanihurst that while he was viceroy, "no busy knave of
them all should trouble him for so worthy a guest as Mr.
Campion." [5]

In the meantime, Campion occupied himself by writing
and dedicating to Leicester his *History of Ireland* (1571),
a short narrative tracing the main outlines of Irish history
from the invasion of Strongbow to 1571, ending with a
stenographic record of two speeches made by Sidney and
Stanihurst before the Irish Parliament in the defense of

[4] R. Simpson, *Edmund Campion*, London, 1896.
[5] *Ibid.*, p. 41.

the proposed University, and embodying the suggestion
that schools be founded in every diocese. Campion's *History,* though rather terse, contains touches of contrast,
quaint and delightful to the modern reader. He scoffs away,
for instance, the legend that Ireland was peopled by Noah's
niece who landed with three men and fifty women, but
gravely argues the question whether the Irish barnacle
which is born of the sea, but hatches to a seagull at ma-
turity, is to be eaten by devout Catholics as flesh or fish;
and, in another place, he solemnly tells us how Irish salmon
catch their tails in their teeth and, letting go suddenly,
flip themselves over the weirs.

An example of his deprecatory tone in dealing with
native education has been noted in the first section of this
study. The theme occurs often. We may accept, therefore,
as substantially true, the usual estimate that Campion's
work is as much a timely argument for the systematic
education of the Irish as it is a serious work of history.

The sketchy character of Campion's history is no doubt
owing in part to the fact that he wrote it under the adverse
conditions of constant flight from Protestant enemies. For
in 1569 Pope Pius V had excommunicated Elizabeth and
declared her subjects free of their allegiance. The constant
intriguing of Mary Queen of Scots, and the report (1571)
that Philip II had submitted to the Pope the tender of the
Irish Crown made to him by Stukeley in the name of the
Irish people, constituted a more substantial threat; Elizabeth met the challenge by laws of increased severity against
English subjects who adhered to the Church of Rome.[6]
Sidney could no longer shield Campion who fled to the
continent, became a Jesuit, and after a short ten years'
career met death on an English scaffold. The details of his
execution are preserved to us in the writings of Anthony
Munday, who, as assistant to Topcliffe the priest-taker,
saw many such sights, and described them with pathologi-

---

[6] R. Simpson, *Edmund Campion,* p. 55.

cal relish. In his *Advertisement and Defence for Truth against her Backbiters* (1581), Munday gives a clear statement of the English feeling against Campion, which it is not off the subject here to quote, expressing as it does the general opinion of all the Mundays to all the Campions of that age:

Campion and companions by procurement of their Heads (Rome, Spain, Italy) came secretly into this Realm to move subjects to renounce their natural obedience, and according to a Bull of the last Pope Pius, publicly to persuade all sorts . . . that her Majesty, by the said Popes excommunication was not the lawful Queen of this Realm, nor that the Subjects were bound to obey any of her laws or Ministers . . . and that they . . . ought to take arms against her Majesty, as in the late rebellion in the North was manifestly by like means put in execution, and as now also lately was notoriously attempted in Ireland, by stirring up the people in the Popes name, and under his standard, to an open general rebellion.

## RICHARD STANIHURST

### 1547–1618

Closely associated with Campion, both in a personal way and in a literary sense, was Richard Stanihurst, sometime commoner of Oxford and member of the Inns of Court, whose writings like those of his friend and tutor are preserved in Holinshed, whose interests, like Campion's, were history and theology, and who, like him, took orders in the Roman Catholic Church. As one tends to group Campion and Stanihurst with Hooker by reason of the interlocking character of their contributions to Holinshed's *Chronicles,* it is now time to define the scope of each one's contribution.

From the preface to the *Chronicles* it appears that Holinshed, casting about in some difficulty to find a suitable chronicle of Ireland, took Campion's *History* as a framework upon which first Hooker and then Stanihurst were invited to build.

The *Chronicle* follows the annals of Flattisbury and his sequelist Marlborough, two early annalists of Ireland, in English, as far as they go, beginning with the legendary mother of the Irish nation, "one Cesara that was niece to Noah (that) hearing her uncle's prophecy, doubted lest the same should come to pass, and therefore determined with certain of her adherents that if she might find a country never yet inhabited and so with sin unspotted, the general sentence of God's wrath should not there take effect. Whereupon rigging a navy she committed herself to the seas, sailing forth till at length she arrived in Ireland, only with three men and fifty women." From this interesting start the chronicle proceeds to the year 1162 where it closes abruptly. At this point, and with an overlay of ten years, Hooker takes up the thread in his translation, *The Irish History composed and written by Giraldus Cambrensis.* This traces the course of the Anglo-Norman invasion from the joint expedition of MacMurrogh and Strongbow in the reign of King Henry II to 1210 in the reign of King John. This in turn was continued, to and through the reign of Henry VIII, by Stanihurst, and was brought to date (1577) by Hooker. The final contribution seems to have been Stanihurst's *Treatise containing an plain and perfect description of Ireland.*

This description is one of the most informative extant writings that relate to Ireland. An interesting passage of Stanihurst's description deals with the preservation of a mangled Chaucerean English in the counties of Fingal and Wexford:

To this day the dregs of the old ancient Chaucer English are kept as well there [Wexford] as in Fingal, as they term a spider, an attercop; a wisp, a wad; a lump of bread, a pocket or pucket; a sillibuck, a copprous; a faggot, a blease or a blaze, for the short burning of it (as I judge); a physician, a leach; a gap, a shard; a base court or quadrangle, a bawen, or rather (as I do suppose) a barton; the household or folks, meanie; sharp, keen; estrange, uncouth; easie, eeth or eafe; a dunghill, a mizen.[7]

7 Stanihurst in *Holinshed*, VI, 4.

Stanihurst, his comments on topography and dialect done, goes on to a description of Irish towns and cities, classes of folk, both English and native Irish, and the manner of their houses, food, and habit. He is unique among the writers of English of his age in giving a catalogue, with brief following critiques, of Celtic writers from St. Patrick down the ages. He is thus the first Irish-English bibliographer and critic of Celtic writings. His style in prose is as lean and stripped as the most exacting could wish, dashed with spicy quotable phrases, and with frequent touches of ironic humor. A contrast greater than that between the simplicity of his prose and the extravagance of his hexameter translation from Vergil is far to seek.

The best contemporary biographical brief of Stanihurst appears in the *New Description of Ireland* by Barnabe Rych who writes:

It is truth he hath run through divers professions, first for a lying learned Historiographer he hath shewed it in his Irish Chronicle.

After that he professed poetry, and among other fictions he took upon him to translate Virgil and stript him out of a velvet gown into a Fool's coat, out of a Latin Heroical verse into an English riffe raffe.

After that I knew him at Antwerp and there he professed Alchemy and took upon him to make gold; from thence he went to Spain and there he became a Physician.

Now I understand he is in the Low Countries about the Arch Duke, and is there become a Massing Priest, and he that when he was at Antwerp failed of his cunning in making gold, hath now gotten a medicine whereby to make God. . . .[8]

Though Stanihurst was Irish by birth, he belongs to English literary history, not alone in verse, but in such prose as deals with Ireland. He belonged to Dublin and to the Pale; his outlook, like his training, was distinctively English.

[8] *New Description of Ireland,* Bjv-ijr.

# IV

## The First Earl of Essex
## in Ulster

### 1573–1576

**I**T is now the place to take leave of Munster for the moment, and the group of chroniclers drawn to Ireland through circumstances related to the first stages of the Desmond wars, and to resume the progress of events in the North.

As we have seen, Shane O'Neill's successor by tribal law, Tirlogh Luineach, had made the gesture of submission before Sir Henry Sidney in 1568. Undeceived by Tirlogh's professions of love for the Queen, the Irish Parliament of 1569—the same which had voted to defeat the project of Dublin University and with it Edmund Campion's hopes —had declared the very name O'Neill extinct and all Ulster forfeit to the Crown, a measure which by English law invalidated every right of real property in Ulster. Henceforth more than ever before, insecurity of life and property, religious persecution and the northward encroachment of shire ground kept the countries of O'Neill and of O'Donnell in constant ferment. The immediate consequence was that Tirlogh Luineach O'Neill joined forces with the Scots of Antrim led by Sorley Boy Mac-Donnell and, not content with harassing rival Celtic chiefs, hovered about the borders of the English Pale. It was to end this nuisance that Elizabeth in 1573 made a private grant of all Ulster to Walter Devereux, first Earl of Essex (1541?–1576) and father to the Queen's later ill-fated favorite of the name, Robert Devereux, second Earl. In return for the grant Essex, having as associates the Lord Rich and the omnipresent Sir Peter Carew, undertook to pacify Ulster and to plant it with English colonists.

28

On 16 August 1573, Essex with his following embarked for Ireland. With the expedition sailed Barnabe Rych with whom we shall deal in a later section, a veteran of the wars in the Low Countries, translator, euphuist and pamphleteer, who crossed in the *Black Bark,* having in his charge the arms and armor of his kinsman Lord Rich. Also of the company was Rych's acquaintance, Barnabe Googe, presumably as an observer for Burghley. It is probable also that with them went Thomas Churchyard who, like Gascoigne, had known Rych in Flanders and in the house at Holdenby of Sir Christopher Hatton, their common patron.

## THOMAS CHURCHYARD

### 1520?–1604

Thomas Churchyard, born at Shrewsbury (c. 1520), received a careful education in classics and in music, but at seventeen he left home for the court with all his patrimony, a little bag of gold. His money spent, he entered the service of Henry Howard, Earl of Surrey. At the death of his patron, Churchyard turned soldier of fortune and traveled to the wars. He served with Sir William Drury in Scotland and, at about thirty, became "servant" to the Earl of Leicester. An unsuccessful wooing sent him to the wars again, in Ireland and elsewhere, whence returning, he married in haste and in haste repented.[1]

Among his voluminous works in verse and prose he has left two short autobiographies in rhyme which, extracted from their respective settings in the first part of *Churchyard's Chips* (1575) and from *Churchyard's Charge* (1580), form the basis of what is known of his adventurous career.

Rhymed apothegms (*The Mirror of Man*), elegies, nar-

[1] P. Bliss, *Bibliographical Miscellanies*, Oxford, 1813, Vol. I.

rative doggerel, as in his autobiographical verse, prose pamphlets of travel and war like the *Chips* and *Charge*, religious pamphlets and military handbooks, all of mediocre quality, pour from his pen with equal fluency, and seldom is the autobiographical touch wanting in one place or another. In the dedicatory epistle to *A Pleasant Description of Court and Wars* (1596), a rhymed paraphrase of what he has overheard spoken on the subject by commanders under whom he has fought, he speaks, for instance, of having served in Ireland under Sir William Fitzwilliam, Sir Anthony St. Leger, Sir James Croft and Sir Henry Sidney, "all these then Deputies." As the deputyships of the four men cover the period 1548–1578, this statement suggests a much more thoroughgoing experience in Ireland than is commonly supposed. At the end of this odd little book Churchyard appends an eulogium to Raleigh. But it is of his experience in Ulster with Essex that he writes most graphically and most at length.

It was with high hopes that the Lord Essex and Lord Rich with their following set out for Ireland. The newly appointed Lord President of Ulster had undertaken to defray in part the cost of the venture, and had received by letters patent a grant of all Antrim except Carrickfergus under conditions which constituted his enormous seignory a kingdom in everything but name. It only remained for him to subdue the legally extinct clans of O'Neill, and their allies, the Argyleshire Scots.[2]

After a rough crossing, Essex and his men landed variously along the eastern and southern coasts in late September and moved northward into Ulster.

Life flowed smoothly for Essex only so long a time as Tirlogh Luineach and Sir Brian McPhelim O'Neill needed to take the English Earl's measure. Tirlogh murdered, pillaged, and burned, and with Sir Brian made common

[2] Bagwell, VII, 240.

cause with the Scotch immigrants by whom the lands of
the Essex grant were already held.[3] Bloody guerilla warfare followed, the character of which is vividly portrayed
by Churchyard:

Now the noble and most bountiful gentleman of England came over
as Governor of Ulster, I mean the Earl of Essex, whose praises no man
in the world can eclipse. Which Earl was accompanied with a goodly
band of horsemen and footmen, he arrived at Carrickfergus. And there
came with him the Lord Rich, Master Henry Knowles and his four
bretheren, Master Michael Carie and Master John Carie, sons to the
Lord of Hunsdon, and Master William Norris and Master John Norris,
two of the eldest sons of the lord Norris, whose carriage and deeds did
shew their noble race. There was likewise one Master Blunt . . . brother
to the Lord Mountjoy and sundry others whose names I have forgotten. . . .

As time did pass and the Earl lay at Carrickfergus news was brought
that one *Neal McBryan Artho* had devised a draught for the killing of
Master Thomas Smith, who was slain by that device. My Lord of Essex
was much moved at that deed and Captain Maltby and his brother were
marvellous sorry for the loss of such a neighbor and good companion.
And swore to revenge his death ere it should be long, as they did when
occasion served therefor. In time . . . the Earl . . . gave John Maltby
leave to go . . . [who] coming into Lakael mustered all the men he
might make, and having a good power . . . practised with one called
Donny Sallow for the catching of Neal Bryan Artho at some advantage. . . . This Donny Sallow . . . went about this matter and
brought such certain news of Neal Bryan Artho's haunt and order of
life that it was an easy thing either to compass him in some danger or
lay hands upon his followers.

And by good occasion Master John Maltby with three score horsemen
and a few footmen . . . made such a slaughter that 35 of Neal Bryan
Artho's men were hacked and slain. Among these men that were slain
was one Con Mackmelog who before caused Master Smith to be eaten
up with dogs after he had been boiled, and the same Con Mackmelog
being slain, was left among wolves five days, and was had into a house
where his friends howled and cried over his dead body so long that by
mischance a great deal of powder caught fire and set the house in a
flame: the Dogs in the town smelling this dead body ran in and took
it out of the house and tore it in pieces and fed upon his carrion flesh

[3] Bagwell, II, 244–245.

openly. Which was a thing to be much marvelled at, and thought to be sent from God for a terror to all tyrants hereafter.[4]

A few experiences like the one described by Churchyard taught the Queen's viceroys that an evicted Irish farmer, living, meant an English colonist, dead.

Churchyard certainly was in Ireland on occasions later than that of the Essex plantation.[5] Among other sketches, he has left us in *A Scourge for Rebels* an account of the first year of the second Desmond rebellion (1579), and of the action at Kinsale, whither he marched with the ensigns of the "hanging deputy," as the Irish called Lord Grey de Wilton, in a company which included Fenton, Rych, Raleigh, and Spenser.

## BARNABE GOOGE [6]

### 1540–1594

Barnabe Googe, a Lincoln man, sometime an undergraduate at Christ's College, Cambridge, and New College, Oxford, went down from the universities to Staples Inn, later becoming retainer to his cousin Sir William Cecil.

His first literary labor, which appeared in 1560, was a translation of the first three books of Manzoli's *Zodiac of Life,* a philosophic essay framed upon the twelve signs of the zodiac. The following year appeared the second edition, comprising six books and dedicated to Cecil. In 1562 the *Eclogues, Epitaphs and Sonnets* were published, and the following year we find that Googe has become a gentleman pensioner to the Queen.[7]

[4] *Churchyard's Choice . . . Campaigns in France, the Netherlands, Scotland and Ireland,* 1579.

[5] *A Scourge for Rebels . . . touching the troubles of Ireland . . . ,* 1584.

[6] B. Googe, *Popish Kingdom or reign of Antichrist,* 1570; ed. with biographical memoir by R. C. Hope, Chiswick Press, London, 1880.

[7] *Ibid.*

The next we hear of Googe is his acceptance of service in Ireland in 1574: Cecil, Lord Burghley, seems to have sent him over as intelligencer or letter-writer to keep Whitehall informed as to the proceedings of Essex.

In 1577 Googe produced the *Four Books of Husbandry*. The author dedicated this work to Sir William Fitzwilliam, then Lord Deputy, and dated it from Kingston, Ireland. From Googe's apology that he had "neither leisure nor quietness at the doing of it, neither after the doing had any time to overlook it" one might infer both regular and arduous employment. The production of such a treatise in dialogue concerning "gardening, grafting and planting" by Googe at this time, fits in very neatly with Hope's conjecture that the author had some connection with the Essex mission of conquest and colonization. That he knew Rych is attested by the phrasing of a prose address prefixed to the first edition of the *Alarm to England* (1578). It is titled, "To my very loving friend Captain Barnabe Rych."

Military experience during the second stage of the Desmond rebellion is suggested by the appointment of Googe to the post of Provost Marshal of Munster in 1582. Three years later he surrendered his patent for this office and returned to England, which he does not again appear to have left. His death occurred in 1594.

With Googe the little group of Elizabethan poets, translators, and pamphleteers who crossed to Ireland prior to 1575 ends. Most of them continued in Ireland until the latter years of the reign; one or two we shall hear of again and again. The present plan of introducing these men in the order of their coming into Ireland, though it be as unsystematic as life itself, has a compensating advantage in this: it allows us to suggest the crossings, interweavings, and parallels of their ways as a more artificial arrangement cannot. If one accepts that definition which classes as literature everything that has been written, and if one applies it to English writing in Ireland of this period, to prose as well as verse, bearing in mind the solidarity of the English official and military castes, one cannot help but conclude that the so-called "Spenser circle" is only one of many interlocking rings.

# V

# *The Desmond Rebellion Second Stage*

## 1575–1583

THE third group of literary adventurers with which this essay deals came to Ireland during the second stage of the Desmond rebellion (1575–1583), and the subsequent plantation of Munster. We accordingly leave the first Earl of Essex, who was soon deserted by Lord Rich and Sir Peter, to wear out the brief remainder of his life in futile excursions against the elusive Tirlogh Luineach O'Neill, while we turn our eyes once more to the southern theatre where a bloody sequel to the first Desmond rebellion is preparing.

The earlier stage of the Desmond rebellion had ended in the submission of James Fitzmaurice Fitzgerald and the liberation and return to Ireland of Gerald Fitzgerald, the Earl, and his brother Sir John of Desmond (1573). For five years thereafter unruly Munster was held in thrall by Sir Henry Sidney.[1] With so strong a grip did Sidney hold it that James Fitzmaurice, ever on the lookout for a Continental alliance but unable to achieve it from Ireland, crossed in 1575 to France, and from there proceeded to the Papal and the Spanish courts in an effort to enlist the aid of Philip II and Pope Gregory XIII. In 1578 his efforts bore fruit in the filibustering expedition led by himself and by the English Catholic, Sir Thomas Stukeley, sometime courtier, pirate and Irish official, who had suffered loss of office at the hands of Sir Peter Carew. The Catholic allies commissioned Stukeley to aid Fitzgerald in organizing a force to land on the Munster coast.[2] A procla-

[1] Joyce, *A Short History of Gaelic Ireland*, pp. 420 ff.
[2] Bagwell, III, 3–6.

mation was published offering amnesty to such Italian brigands as should come in and volunteer their services for the invasion of Ireland, and by this ingenious recruiting device, a force of a thousand men soon gathered at Civita Veccia.[3] Favoring winds sped the ships west and north, but at Lisbon, owing, it is thought, to the persuasion of Sebastian of Portugal,[4] Stukeley formed the design of a buccaneering venture against the king of Morocco. The result was a division of the fleet, Stukeley turning south, while Fitzgerald with two papal emissaries, Allen and Sanders, and a small mixed following in three ships, held his course and landed on the coast of Kerry the latter part of July.

Hardly had Fitzgerald and his men come out of their ships when they began to experience the reverses that were to end in the complete collapse of the Geraldine cause. The Burkes of Castleconnel killed Fitzgerald on a sordid charge of horsetheft, and the command fell to Sir John Desmond, against whom Sir William Drury (then viceroy), and after him, Sir Nicholas Maltby, took the field.[5] Thus, what had begun as formal aid to the Irish cause from Spain and the Holy See resolved itself into a hopeless struggle of the dwindled forces under Desmond's command against Irish enemies on the one hand, and English governors on the other. In early September, Sir Nicholas Maltby lay at Kilmallock with a large force at his command.[6]

Here the English forces concentrated for what was to be the final rout of the Desmond Geraldines. Hither, to reinforce Maltby's cavalry, came a levy of six hundred veterans from the Low countries, "halbadiers, cabiners and pikemen" in blockish bands, marching south from Dublin. Flank patrols and flying outposts scoured the country, driv-

[3] Bagwell, III, 5–6.
[4] *Ibid.*, II, 7; Joyce, p. 446.
[5] *Ibid.*, III, 23.
[6] *Ibid.*, III, 29.

ing the cattle away from miserable farmsteads, and laying waste with plow, harrow, and torch what little the fields produced, until the wake of the English march lay bleak as desert land.

Driven from their farms, their wives and children butchered outright or dying of famine or disease, Irishmen flocked to the Geraldine camp in the hills to the north of Monaster.[7] Desmond commanded these Irish, and with him was the Jesuit, Sanders, and the papal emissary, Allen, who bore a silken banner, charmed to infallibility by a papal blessing. In their respective positions the two armies waited, gathering strength for the action of September 29.

To Maltby's headquarters on the eve of the battle came Barnabe Rych with a note from Sir Francis Walsingham and the request that he be given command of one of Maltby's companies.[8] Out of his experience at Monaster, Rych has left a vivid account of how the Geraldines were cut to pieces, how Desmond and Sanders fled through the woods at nightfall, and of how Allen died on the field.[9]

Through the following year, Rych continued to serve with Maltby during the reduction of Munster, and afterwards with Lord Grey in his march to the valley of Glenmalure and Smerwick, together with a celebrated band of adventurers among whom were Geoffrey Fenton, now Secretary for Ireland, Edmund Spenser, secretary to Gray, John Hooker and Captain Walter Raleigh, at whose command the garrison of six hundred Spanish and Irish defenders at Smerwick were put to the sword—an act approved by Hooker and Spenser alike. Probably to this period also belongs John Derricke, of whose life virtually nothing is known, aside from the fact that he is said to have been a protégé of Sir Henry Sidney, and a friend to Sir Philip which, if true, makes another pebble for the

[7] Bagwell, III, 28 ff.
[8] Sir N. Maltby to Walsingham, 10 Sept. 1579 (S.P.I., Vol. 79, 17).
[9] New Description of Ireland, 1610.

Spenser-Sidney pool. His book, the *Image of Ireland* (written c. 1578, printed 1581), is in two divisions, the first depicting Ireland in the medium of pastoral allegory, and the second giving a rather more serious description of the woodkern or forest dwellers.

## JOHN DERRICKE [10]

### fl. 1578

Derricke dedicates his book to Sir Philip Sidney. In the dedicatory epistle, he acknowledges his indebtedness for past favors to Sir Henry Sidney, whose praises throughout he sings. What these favors were we are left to conjecture.

*The Image* is an odd little essay in tumbling measure, illustrated with twelve elaborate woodcuts. These cuts are valuable as showing how wide was the variety of costume in use among both Englishmen and Irishmen of that age, and as lending color to the surmise of the editor that Derricke may have been an engraver with some official connection. Certain it is that, in a tantalizing passage of negative autobiography, he excludes every vocation but the arts.

> I was no fit Astronomer,
>     to treat upon the Stars:
> Nor yet trained up in Marses court,
>     to tell of bloody wars.
> I was no famous Orator,
>     nor crafty man of Law:
> Which from a but of Muscadine,
>     a tun of Malmsies draw.
> Nor yet recounted excellent,
>     in those high mist'ries seven:
> By which I might upon mine oath
>     tell what is done in heaven.
> I was not of God Neptune's Court,
>     as Pirates be on seas:

[10] *The Image of Ireland, with a Discovery of the Woodkern*, 1581. Ed. J. Small, 1883.

I deemed it far a better life,
   (though poor) to live at ease.
I was not skilful in their trades
   which give out gold to gain:
No, no, I dare avouch such saints
   my pouch did never stain.
Nor yet with Merchant venturers,
   (those were too high for me):
Unneath to shew their famous sleight,
   unquainted might I be:
I found not in me verily,
   of writers that's required:
How might I then perform the thing,
   my soul and heart desired? [11]

When we learn that Derricke's heart's desire was the satirical description of the Ulster woodkern, and the eulogy of Sir Henry Sidney, the only means he seems to have left himself are those of the graphic arts, yet here again the prevailing print-signature of F.D. and not I.D. remains to be explained.

Derricke begins with panegyric in verse of English monarchs from King Arthur to Elizabeth, "who not only hath continued in ye course of her Father, by suppressing ye pope, but with more severity hath holden his nose down to the grindstone, as by continual grinding it is almost worn out to the gristle and bare stumps."

And so to Ireland which in the first part of his book the author represents as a society of hibernian nymphs and fauns, constituted by Mars, Apollo, and Jupiter, serpents and toads being banished to perfect the incongruous paradise. This is undoubtedly a broad burlesque upon legendary Irish history. The habit and life of the woodkern are foreordained by a Jovian decree, and the English are warned of the danger of miscegenation in terms of fantastic inappositeness, a good example of which follows in Derricke's description of the wood nymphs at play:

[11] *Image of Ireland.*

These do invite the Murm'ryng brooks,
   these dive and rise again:
And bathing in their sweet delights,
   so long they do remain,
Till Cupid toll'th his sacring bell
   to enter other Rites:
Ah would't revive a man half dead?
   to see those naked sprites?

Jupiter now gives commands for the marshaling of the kern:

The order of the Irish karnes apparel, is here allowed by Jupiter being first found out by Apollo.

Let therefore little Mountain Gods
   a troupe (as they may spare:)
Of breachless men at all assays,
   both levy and prepare.
With Mantles down unto the Shoe
   to lap them in by night:
With spears and swords and little darts
   to shield them from despight.
And let some have their breeches close,
   to nimble things annexed:
With safer means to dance the Bogs,
   when they by foes are vexed.
With glibbed heads like Mars him self,
   their malice to express:
With ireful hearts and bloody hands
   soon prone to wickedness.
Jove spake. Twas done and I suppose,
   then Serpents were dismist:
And sent away, which to be true,
   now credit if ye list.

As the essay progresses, broad satire and burlesque are by degrees modulated. The latter half of Part One touches upon the richness of Ireland in natural resources, of Irish hawks, horses, cattle; it proceeds to a passage of bitter invective directed at the kern, and closes with verses of praise addressed to Sir Henry Sidney. Part Two is given almost wholly to the portraiture of a "type" battle between English and Irish: it describes the orderly stand of the

For if his ballaunce once be mou'de, reuenge on them to take,
Which doe our soueraigne Princes rage, like beastly beastes forsake:
Tys not the cruell stormy rage, not gathered force of those
For yet the crooked crabtree lookes, of greasye gibbed foes,
Can make him to reuoke the thing, his honor hath pretended
But that Dame Iustice must procede, 'gaynst those that haue offended.

9

For Mars will see the finall end, of trayt'rous waged warres,
To plucke the hartes of Rebells downe, that lately pearst the starres.
To yelde them guerdon for desertes, by rigour of his blade,
And with the same to gall their hartes, which such vproxes haue made.
Loe where it is in open sight, most perfect to be seene
Which sheweth the fatall end aright, of rebells to our Queene.

English and the impetuous massed charge of the Irish, led by their pipers and heartened by the characteristic warcry of "Oobooboo," later anglicized to "Hubbub." The English are, of course, victorious and the Irish horse and kern wheel and retire to their hidden strongholds in the wood.

## LODOWICK BRYSKETT

### fl. 1571–1611

Lodowick Bryskett, poet and translator, protégé of Sir Henry Sidney and of Lord Grey, enjoyed in common with Barnabe Rych the friendship of Sir Francis Walsingham. At Trinity College, Cambridge, he met Sir Philip Sidney and, with him, he toured Europe from 1572 to 1575, thus favored perhaps, owing to his Italian parentage and consequent fluency in the language. On his return a clerkship was found for him in the Chancery for the Faculties in Ireland, and thenceforward his career closely parallels that of Spenser, with whom he was associated in both official and personal relations, and to whom he relinquished his office eleven years later. Both served for years as civil servants, both undertook Irish lands—Bryskett in Wexford, Spenser in Cork—and both suffered from the raids of Tyrone adherents in 1598. We note in passing that the appointment of Geoffrey Fenton in 1581 to succeed Sir John Challoner as Secretary to Ireland appears to have been the cause of Bryskett's disgruntled retirement from official life, as Bryskett had vainly petitioned Burghley for the appointment as soon as Challoner's illness gave evidence of being fatal.[12]

Bryskett's chief literary work is his translation from the Italian of Baptista Giraldo's philosophical treatise, *A Discourse of Civil Life* (written c. 1582). It appears from the prose address prefixed to this work, so long delayed in

[12] H. R. Plomer and T. P. Cross, *The Life and Correspondence of Lodowick Bryskett*, pp. 17 ff. 1927.

publication, that Lord Grey supported his protégé in his suit for the Secretaryship. Addressing Lord Grey, Bryskett says, "It pleased his Lordship to appoint [him] after the death of John Challoner, her Majesty's Secretary of Ireland, to that place," and though the Lord Grey's intention took not effect, the repulse enabled him to do a greater favor still in making it possible for Bryskett to resign the office of Clerk of the Council and withdraw to the quietness of his studies. Bryskett accordingly dedicates to Gray the first fruit of those studies, and describes the work as having grown out of a meeting of friends who in the course of his slight illness had come to visit him at his cottage near Dublin. The friends Bryskett mentions are, Dr. Long, Primate of Ardmagh, Sir Robert Dillon, Knight, Mr. Dormer, the Queen's solicitor, Captain Christopher Carlyle, Thomas Norris, Captain Warham St. Leger, Captain Nicholas Dawtrey, Edmund Spenser, and Thomas Smith, Apothecary.[13]

Bryskett remarks before the company that he envies the happiness of the Italians who have popularized moral philosophy by translating and explaining Plato and Aristotle in the vulgar tongue. He wishes English writers had done or would do the same, and challenges Spenser, who replies that he has already undertaken the *Faerie Queene* to the same effect. The argument of the book follows, its structure a conversation of three days during which philosophical discussion takes place, the main premises being substantially those of Davies' *Nosce Teipsum*.

This well-known passage from the Bryskett preface is here again alluded to because, through one or another of the persons named in it, a thread of association may be traced that links—slenderly be it confessed—every writer with which this study has to do.

Lastly, there is a suggestion that Bryskett may have

---

[13] *A Discourse of Civil Life: Containing the Ethick part of Morall Philosophie.* London, 1606. Aiijrv.

collaborated with Rych in translating the eight *novelle*
which form the latter's *Farewell to Military Profession*—
one of which has been considered Shakespeare's source for
*Twelfth Night*. Among the prefatory matter of the British
Museum copy (Malone 613 of the 1606 edition), Rych
writes concerning the collection: "The third (*Of Nicander
and Lucilla*), the fourth (*Of Fineo and Fiamma*) and the
sixth (*Of Gonzales and his virtuous wife Agatha*): are
Italian histories written likewise for pleasure by Master
L. B." And in the margin by this is a note in Edmond
Malone's hand: "Probably Lodowick Bryskett."

Now to go back for a moment to the subject of literary associations which are traceable through the historic
Bryskett gathering: It was the father of Sir Warham
St. Leger, Sir Anthony, at whose invitation Churchyard
came to Ireland to serve against Shane O'Neill. Churchyard knew Barnabe Rych and had used his notes. To Rych's
*Alarm to England* Barnabe Googe had written the prose
epistle and prefixed laudatory verse in 1578. Rych had
known Campion's sometime disciple, Stanihurst, at Antwerp. Rych, moreover, had dedicated his *Farewell to Military Profession* to his friend and patron, Sir Christopher
Hatton, who numbered among other protégés George
Gascoigne, Churchyard and Spenser. With Spenser's the
name of Sir Philip Sidney comes naturally to mind, and
thus the circle closes.

## EDMUND SPENSER

### 1552?–1599

The career of Edmund Spenser in Ireland has been dealt
with by scholars to such an extent, and in such detail, that
an unassuming suggestion that other writers of the time
may not only have been present and have written, but that
they may have been read as well, is one of the ends of this
essay. For our purposes it is enough to mention his *View of*

*the Present State of Ireland*, a description, in form of dialogue, of Ireland at the time of the Desmond wars. This
tract, published in 1592, reflects the experience and obser-
vation of twelve years in official circles. We might add, by
the way, that it is strikingly paralleled by Barnabe Rych's
later *Anothomy of Ireland*, a MS dialogue addressed to King
James; but is, of course, of earlier date, more graphic, less
interested, and more searching.

Like Rych, Spenser denounces as the chief evils of the
English administration the sale of offices, protections, and
pardons by the highest officials of the kingdom; bribes
taken for appointments to county offices; shares of bishop-
rics exacted as the price of nominating bishops; and the
selling of licenses for the export of prohibited wares. The
chief social evil and a basic cause of all abuses, to the poet's
way of thinking, is the inevitable hibernization of the English settlers. Let the Irish be exterminated, therefore, the
priests hanged or deported, and let corrupt official practices
in Ireland be thoroughly purged.

Over and above his penetrating and graphic, if unsympathetic, interpretation of the social and political Ireland
of his day, Spenser, like Raleigh, affords an illustration of
the resident landed proprietor who "undertook" forfeited
Irish land.

Through friendships formed at Pembroke Hall, Cambridge, the poet was recommended to the Earl of Leicester,
and was employed by the Earl on courier service. Possibly
through Leicester, or through Sir Philip Sidney, Spenser was
appointed secretary to Lord Grey de Wilton on the eve of
his departure as Lord Deputy to Ireland in 1580.

In November, Spenser accompanied Grey in the march
to Smerwick in Kerry, and he has given a vivid account of
the action at Smerwick, and of the desolation that followed
the march of the English army. About the same time he
met Raleigh, and formed a friendship with Bryskett from
whom, as we have seen, seven years later he obtained by

purchase the succession to the office of clerk of the government council in Munster.[14] In the meantime, while serving
as clerk of Degrees and Recognizances in the Irish Court of
Chancery, he received a lease of the lands and abbey of Enniscorthy in county Wexford which, as we have touched on
in another place, Stanihurst writes of as having preserved
in its dialect many survivals of Chaucerian English. It is
pleasant to play with the thought that Spenser may here
have been brought into contact with the vital, everyday use
of an archaic idiom to which already his academic Chaucer-
worship inclined him.

In 1582 Spenser received a six-year lease of Lord Balting-
las' house in Dublin [15] and, in August of the same year, a
lease of New Abbey, county Kildare, where he often stayed.
In May 1583, and again in July 1584, he acted as a commis-
sioner for the musters, county Kildare, a post which brought
him again into contact with military affairs. On 22 June
1588, he resigned the clerkship of the court of Chancery in
Dublin, acting for Lodowick Bryskett in the post of Clerk
of the Council of Munster. Sir Thomas Norris, another of
the gathering mentioned by Bryskett in his preface, was
then acting President.

Two years earlier (1586), the property of the Earls of
Desmond in Munster had been declared forfeit, and the
policy of planting English colonists on a large scale definitely decided on. The Earl and his chief followers had been
attainted and some 600,000 acres declared forfeit to the
Crown.[16] In the articles for the "undertakers" (grantees
who "undertook" to transport a stated minimum number
of English farmers and artisans to their grants of land),
Spenser was credited with 3,028 acres (27 June 1586). The
final patent securing his title to this property for three years
was passed 26 October 1591. On the property was the old

[14] D. N. B.
[15] P. Henley, *Spenser in Ireland*, pp. 38 ff.
[16] D. N. B.

castle of Kilcolman, three miles from Doneraile, County Cork. The subsequent history of Spenser at Coleraine belongs to the story of the Tyrone rebellion of 1597–1598. Now let us turn back a little and bring to date the career of Spenser's neighbor and fellow speculator in Irish land, Captain Walter Raleigh.

## WALTER RALEIGH

### 1552?–1618

A Devonshire man and commoner of Oriel College, Oxford,[17] Walter Raleigh became a soldier and, after service in the Huguenot armies at Jarnac and Montcour, came to Ireland at the outbreak of the Desmond wars. Through Sidney a protégé of Walsingham's, he used Ireland as a stepping stone to higher favor. As one of the commission that condemned to death James Fitzmaurice Fitzgerald, cousin of the Earl of Desmond, and through his gallantry at Smerwick,[18] he made a name for himself in the space of a single year. An illuminating glimpse of Raleigh in the field appears from the following anecdote by Hooker in *Holingshed*:

Captain Raleigh, notwithstanding that the Lord Deputy had raised his camp at Rekell, and was gone toward the fort, yet he tarried and stayed behind, minding to practise some exploit. For it was not unknown to him that it was a manner among the Irish kerns that whensoever any English camp was dislodged and removed, they would after those departures come to those camps to take what they there found to be left. Thus therefore lying, and keeping himself very close, tarried and abode the coming of the said kerns, who suspecting no such trap to be laid for them, came after their manners and old usages to the said place and there took their pleasure, who when they were in their security, the captain and his men came upon them and took them all. Among them was one who carried and was laden with wythes, which they used in place of halters, and being demanded what he would do with them, and why

17 D. N. B.
18 Bagwell, III, 75.

he carried them, gave answer that they were to hang up English churls, for so they call Englishmen. "Is it so?" (quoth the captain), "well, they shall now serve for an Irish kern," and so commanded him to be hanged up with one of his own wythes.[19]

In December 1581 Raleigh was sent to England with despatches from Colonel Zouch, the new governor of Munster. From this visit to court his rapid rise to favor and power may be dated, for he was able to lay before Burghley a plan for ending the Desmond rebellion which met with the Lord Treasurer's approval.[20] The plan was to put the Earl's pardon and restoration entirely out of the question, and to receive to mercy and service all those chiefs who were actuated more by fear of their neighbor Earl than by disaffection to the Queen. Seven hundred men in garrison would do the rest.[21] Desmond's hereditary enemy, the Earl of Ormonde, was to be chiefly relied on for bringing back the still rebellious chiefs to their allegiance. This reasoning prevailed, and the governorship of Munster with large powers to act against the enemy of his house was given to Ormonde. Within the year the Earl of Desmond was taken, killed, and his head sent to the Queen. Thus ended the final stage of the Desmond war.

In 1586, the year of the official attainder of the Desmond estates in Munster, Raleigh obtained a grant of forty thousand acres in counties Cork, Waterford, and Tipperary.[22] Raleigh (now Sir Walter, for he had been knighted in 1584) did plant a number of English families upon his Irish estates, but his residence in Ireland ceased about this time, though he revisited Ireland on occasion, witness his visit to Kilcolman in 1589. But as his favor at court grew and his other interests multiplied, his visits to Ireland became infrequent until, in the middle nineties, we find him disposing of his Irish holdings one by one.

[19] Hooker in *Holinshed*, VI, 487.
[20] Bagwell, III, 101.
[21] *Ibid*.
[22] *D. N. B.*

Raleigh's literary work belongs to England exclusively. His benefaction to Irish culture was not literary, it was dietary; for to him go the laurels for first cultivating in his garden at Youghal the new-imported white potato. His career in Ireland, like Spenser's, illustrates the manner of the plantations and of the wars that accompanied them. To Ireland Raleigh owed in no small degree the beginnings of his long and brilliant career at court as surely as it was to Ireland that Robert Devereux, second Earl of Essex, owed his ruin.

# VI

# *The Munster Plantation*

## 1586–1599

*T*HE defeat of the Desmond Geraldines and the suppres-
sion of rebellion in Munster and Leinster ended in the
virtual extinction of the house of Desmond in the person
of the Earl who died at the hands of Ormonde Butlers in
1583. The forfeiture to the Crown of the vast estates
formerly owned by the Earl and his followers was confirmed by the Act of Attainder of 1586, though we have
noted in passing that even before this, Raleigh, Spenser,
and Bryskett were in possession of Irish holdings. In 1586
a general proclamation was made in England, inviting
gentlemen to undertake the plantation of the escheated
lands under conditions which amounted to gift. Estates
were offered at twopence the acre, rent free for the first
five years.[1] Every "undertaker" pledged himself to settle
one English tenant family to every 140 acres of his estate,
and the total acreage granted individual undertakers
ranged between four and twelve thousand acres. Irish tenants were barred.[2]

Many of those who undertook Irish lands remained
absentee speculators.[3] Raleigh with forty-two thousand
acres in Cork, and Spenser with twelve thousand acres are,
of course, the most obvious exceptions. But in spite of the
liberal terms offered, the scheme in the main was a failure.
English farmers and artisans did not come over in sufficient
numbers, and the "undertakers" received the native Irish
everywhere in violation of the conditions of their grants.[4]
Some English did come, but were so harassed by the dis-

[1] Mahoney, p. 72; Joyce, p. 461.
[2] Small, J. (ed.), *Image of Ireland.*
[3] Mahoney, p. 73.
[4] Spenser, *View*; Davies, *Discovery.*

possessed Irish, that most of them returned to England. In the end more than half of the escheated estates returned to the possession of their original owners, for no others could be found to take them.[5]

It is easy to see that the seeds of failure lay in the very conditions of the grants, which arbitrarily settled English colonists on the farms of Irish irregular soldiers for whom no provision had been made. The Irish were thus put in the position of fighting or starving; while the English, soon learning that the only good kern was a dead kern, solved the problem of a double population by the systematic extermination of the native Irish. When we consider how to the opposition of tribal versus feudal law the fanatic bitterness of religious persecution came to be added, the genesis of a racial hatred strong enough to bridge the centuries is hardly to be wondered at. From 1585 until the final subjugation of Ireland under Mountjoy twenty years later, the process of plantation went forward throughout the South, but all resembled in their main features the Munster plantation, as the Munster resembled the Ulster plantation before it. From first to last all were accomplished at a fearful cost both to native Irish and to English colonists.

The interest of the great "undertakers" was naturally mercenary, and what social data had any grace of human interest appear to have lain in despatch, and not in published form, except in the writings of Robert Payne, who is interesting as having been sent to Ireland as the agent of a group of twenty-five colonists to scout conditions before those interested should commit themselves to the plantation venture. Payne's pamphlet, *A Brief Description of Ireland Made in this Year 1589 by Robert Payne Unto xxv of his partners for whom he is undertaker there*, is also interesting as suggesting by the words of its title a private syndicate for colonization.

[5] Bagwell, III, 138 ff; Joyce, p. 462.

## ROBERT PAYNE

### fl. 1590

Payne, a Nottinghamshire man, subsequently describing himself of Payne's End, Cork[6], was, like Gervase Markham who came after him, a writer of books relating to husbandry, the making of dew-ponds,[7] the draining of flooded lands, and the art of surveying. In consequence of the inducements offered Englishmen to settle in Munster, Payne and twenty-five of his neighbors planned to remove there. But before risking life and fortune among the wild Irish, Payne went over to make a report on the situation. The result was the *Brief Description*.

The pamphlet answers the questions in the mind of the prospective average colonist and, on the whole, it paints a favorable, if not idyllic, picture the main outlines of which are these:

"The better sort of Irish," writes Payne in a vein of naïve optimism, "are very civil, hospitable and honestly given and bring up their children to learning. They keep faith, are quick-witted and of good bodily constitution, and form themselves daily more and more after English manners. Nothing is more pleasing to them than to hear of good Justices placed amongst them."

Some fear that the Spanish will enter the land and that the Irish will support them, but "their reception in 1588–89 showed how they affect Spanish government, slaying them like dogs in such plentiful manner that their garments went about the country to be sold as cheap as beast's skins."

Payne now turns to his special interest, agriculture, prices, and the state of the plantation, giving much practical data that reads rather like a Chamber of Commerce report.

[6] T. A. Smith (ed.), R. Payne, *Brief Description*, v. biog. pref.
[7] Ames, *Typographical Antiquities*, III, 1662.

The soil is fertile and suited to the cultivation of every form of grain and fruit that England yields. Good timber is so straight and easily riven "that a simple workman with a brake axe will cleave a great oak to boards of less than one inch thick, fourteen inches broad and fifteen foots in length," such a board selling for twopence halfpenny.

There is great plenty of iron ore, especially of the kind called bog mine; of lead ore, and wood sufficient to maintain iron and lead works (with good husbandry) forever.

A barrel of wheat and a barrel of bay salt containing three bushels and a half of Winchester measure is sold for four shillings, malt, peas, beans for 2s 8d, barley 2s 4d, oats for 20s; a fresh salmon worth in London 10s for 6d; 24 herrings or 6 mackerels, 6 sea breams, a fat hen, 30 eggs, a fat pig, one pound of butter or two gallons of new milk, for a penny. A red deer without the skin sells for 2s 6d; a fat beef for 13s 4d; a fat mutton for 18d.

There is a plentifulness of wild swans, cranes, pheasants, partridges, heathcocks, plovers green and gray, curlews, woodcocks, rails and all other fowl. A dozen quail may be had for threepence, woodcocks for 4d. About the coast, oysters, mussels, and cockles are to be had for the taking up. In short, "You may keep a better house in Ireland for fifty pounds a year than in England for two hundred pounds a year. . . . All your commodities you may transport from the sea side from the county of Cork . . . to England for eightpence the hundredweight, so that you make the same ready about St. Andrew's tide [30 November] when the herring fishers go home from Ireland."

The worse sort of undertakers charge exorbitant rates, preferring Irish tenants who will pay their rents and other tribal dues besides, but the better sort favor the English and offer 300 acres in fee farm, or 400 by lease for 100 years at sixpence the acre.

Payne now enters a note on the currency which has the authentic tinkle of modern financial mysticism:

Most of the coin in Ireland, and that which the people generally desire is base money made of copper or brass, they will not change you an Angel into that money without fourpence gains: I would to God her Majesty would coin five hundred thousand marks of the same, and lend it to the English merchants gratis for two year, to be employed there in madder, woad, rape, hops, hemp, flax, and such other commodities as might set some great number of our English men to work: by which means (in my judgment) the land might be very well peopled, her Majesty disburdened of a great part of her charge there, the merchants made great gainers, and yet at the two years end pay her Majesty her full sum in current English money for that base metal, whereby her Majesty might gain at least 200 thousand pounds without hurt to any, and good to many thousands.

The *Brief Description* is, it is true, of no great account either as writing or as history, but it is the sole printed account of the Tudor plantations from the viewpoint of the average colonist, as distinguished from the landed, official, and military castes. Apparently Payne did not last long in Ireland. In ironic contrast to his guileless optimism was the true condition of affairs in the Kingdom. To illustrate this we must turn again to the involved and perplexing vagaries of Irish history.

Connaught and Munster during the viceroyalty of Sir John Perrott (1585–1588) kept the peace of exhaustion, but while the work of plantation went forward in west and south, the spirit of rebellion began again to stir in the Ulster stronghold of the rival Celtic houses of O'Donnell in the west and O'Neill in Tyrone.

It has been said that territorial encroachment, the religious question and the corruption of the Anglican prelacy appointed to clerical, and sometimes civil, office were main and constant factors in northern unrest. Into this the element of treachery had entered when in 1587 Sir John Perrott arranged the kidnapping of the young Hugh Roe O'Donnell, cousin of Hugh Roe O'Neill of Tyrone, and held him hostage against the rebellion he saw so clearly in the making. By this act he drew on himself the anger and

distrust of the North and united the two great rival houses
of O'Donnell and O'Neill whose traditional division had
been a source of strength to the Crown.[8] The now aged but
still elusive Tirlogh Luineach had been confirmed as chief
of Tyrone for life, but Hugh Roe, Matthew's son and lineal
second Earl of Tyrone, now a man of forty, had assumed
the actual active leadership of Tyrone by 1585. Hugh Roe
O'Donnell of Tyrconnel, made chief of his clan in 1592
after his second escape from Dublin castle, though young,
promised to equal in qualities of leadership his remarkable
cousin by marriage, O'Neill.[9] Perrott's policy, uniting the
two as it did, was as unhappy as had been Sidney's support
of Carew twelve years before with the resulting alliance
of Desmond with Ormonde. The result in Ulster, though
not so instant, was equally certain; for Hugh Roe O'Neill,
like his uncle Shane, was a jealous steward of his lands and
a devout Roman Catholic who stood first and last for
political independence and the freedom of Ulster to worship as it chose. Though the Tyrone rebellion did not break
into open flame till 1594, the spirit of revolt steadily
gained ground. This was especially true of the decade following the repulse of the Armada in 1588, for the Armada, as Bagwell points out, was in essence a religious
crusade, and as such Elizabeth and her councillors understood it. In consequence, anti-Catholic feeling rose to fever
heat. A point of friction closely related to the religious
question was the type of Englishman often preferred in
the Irish Church to offices and livings which were, in view
of Ireland's ancient Catholic tradition, simple sinecures
floated on Irish taxes.

[8] Moryson, *Itinerary* II, 186 ff.
[9] Joyce, pp. 465 ff.

## NATHANIEL BAXTER

### fl. 1606

A minor illustration of such preferment was the case
of Nathaniel Baxter, poet and Puritan writer of tracts,
sometime Fellow of Christ Church, Cambridge, and tutor
to Sir Philip Sidney, who seems, like many of the men
already dealt with, to have come to Ireland by favor of one
or another of his patrons, the Sidneys.

On 23 May 1592, Baxter became warden of St. Mary's
College, Youghal. Originally a Jesuit college, the warden-
ship of St. Mary's had become a sinecure, for the college
itself had been razed in successive sackings of the town by
both Irish and English in the course of the Munster rebellions.[10] Baxter continued at Youghal as near neighbor to
Spenser, and Raleigh is known to have stayed at Youghal
from time to time. His visit to Spenser in 1598 and view of
the *Faerie Queene* has been, perhaps, too often alluded to,
yet here is one of the provocative groupings which we have
met before in the course of this study and will meet again.
There is no evidence to connect Baxter either with Raleigh
or with the Spenser group; but, as neighbor to Spenser and
sometime tutor to Sidney, there is every likelihood that
some connection there was. And it is a fact worth noting
that, when in 1598 Baxter was forced to surrender his office, during the time of grace allowed him, the college
revenues and the warden's house were hastily demised to
the same Sir Thomas Norris named by Bryskett as of the
party gathered at his cottage near Dublin.[11]

Baxter holds an insignificant niche among the minor
poets of the age by virtue of his connection with Sidney
and his poem "Sir Philip Sidney's Ourania" (1602), a baga-
telle with autobiographical touches relating to the friendship of Astrophel and "Tergaster."

[10] D. N. B.
[11] *Ibid.*

*Sir Philip Sidney's Ourania, That is, Endymion's Song and Tragedy, containing all Philosophy. Written by N.B. 1606*, is attributed by Hunter to "Rev. N. Baxter, a clergyman, Incumbent of Troy, author of some works of divinity, who had been tutor to Sir Philip Sidney and whose poetical name was Endymion." [12] Baxter dedicates his poem to an impressive list of prominent ladies, but chiefly, "To his ever-honored Lady and Mistress Arcadian Cynthia, Maria Pembrokiana."

*Ourania*, to judge by Corser's extracts, seems to have been a discursive philosophical essay treating of "the universe and whatever therein may be found" in heroic rhyming couplets. Cynthia becomes the poet's patroness, and urges him "sacred notes mongst learned men to chant." Thus encouraged he takes:

> A subject fit for Sidney's eloquence,
> High Chaucer's vein and Spenser's influence.

Concerning more specific aim or design we are left in the dark. One suggestive stanza there is, spoken by the shade of Sidney (Astrophel) who appears to the poet:

> Art thou (quoth he) my Tutor Tergaster?
> He answered, yea: such was my happy chance.
> I grieve (quoth Astrophel) at thy disaster;
> But fates deny me learning to advance.
> Yet Cynthia shall afford thee maintenance.
> My dearest Sister, keep my Tutor well,
> For in his element he doth excel.

This, assuredly, has the ring of invoking the past to sustain the warmth of bounty in the breast of his patroness.

[12] J. Hunter, *New Illustrations of . . . Shakespeare*, 1845; T. Corser, *Collectanea Anglo-Poetica*, 1883.

## BARNABE RYCH

### 1540?–1617

Baxter left Ireland in 1599, and it was in England that he wrote the verse for which he is chiefly remembered. His Irish career illustrates the sort of sinecure placement which brought the Anglican clergy into odium with both Irish and English Irish. But if we change the scene from Cork to Dublin, we have a much more dynamic example of the wholesale abuse of church benefices which estranged even the Anglo-Irish, illustrated in the activities of Adam Loftus, Lord Chancellor and former Dean of St. Patricks; and his brother by marriage, Thomas Jones, the Bishop of Meath, two clever and politic churchmen, always suspected of sharp dealings, sometimes closely pressed, but never quite pinned down. The charges against Loftus and Jones are especially thoroughgoing because an informer named Robert Legg [13] seems to have been expressly authorized by Cecil to investigate them. Associated with Legg we find Barnabe Rych. Their joint activities not only throw an interesting light upon the ethics of Loftus and Jones, but constitute an unique human-interest record of the Tudor informer at work.[14]

The first document that deals with the Loftus-Jones investigation is a letter from Loftus to Burghley dated 27 June 1592. Incidentally it is the sole extant contemporary "character" of Rych, and hence worth quoting in full:

Barnabe Rych, a gentleman, one of her Majesty's pensioners in the kingdom, whom albeit in my life I never offended, yet am I advised by some of his own confederacy that for these twelve months past and more, he and some others, have been strict observers of all my doings, and have secretly collected and booked some accusations both against myself and some other of my bretheren of the clergy here: which, as he him self hath commonly reported, were delivered to her Majesty's

[13] Robert Legg to Burghley, S. P. for I. v. 165. 18.
[14] Cf. Appendix II.

hands at his last being in England, the cause of which his dealing and practise against us I cannot ascribe to any other thing but to the malicious disposition of some papists and atheists in this kingdom (with whom for the most part Rych is conversant) who (to disgrace our persons for our profession's sake) have as I conceive raised him as another Martin to sow the seeds of sedition by this godly course, being a man of himself very needy, by nature immodest and subject to many and very gross infirmities, who for a further manifestation of his malicious heart against me very lately in the street of Dublin assaulted one of my poor servingmen and after some spiteful words used against him because he was my servant, almost even at my heels with his drawn sword cut off one of his fingers and desperately wounded him, which outrageous part I patiently put up and gave straight charge to all my servants to forbear to revenge, hoping that in time Rych would more advisedly consider of his behaviour . . . towards me. Nevertheless I am now lately given to understand that Mr. Rych, not yet satisfied with the injuries he has done, is suddenly departed into England with purposes, as himself hath reported, to burst forth into some exclamations with me and some others of this clergy.[15]

Four days later Loftus wrote a second anxious letter to Burghley, begging to have a note of the charges lodged against him. The substance of the letter is this:

I cannot conceive from whom any accusations against myself or the Bishop of Meath could proceed unless it be from Barnabe Rych, or from one Legg, a late officer of her Majesty's exchequer . . . a man . . . noted and detected of great lewdness, dishonesty and corruption, both which being joined in league of friendship with one Pypho, a renowned Atheist, and a most filthy liver . . . [These], wanting not encouragement from the papists of this country, have been for this year past and more secret collectors and lookers on of matters against us.[16]

Through July and August Loftus and Meath continued to solicit Burghley for a copy of the articles charged against them by Rych and Legg, and their efforts in the end bore fruit; for in a despatch from Rathfarnan, dated

---

[15] Loftus to Burghley, S. P. for I. 27 June 1592. Rych tells quite a different story in his letter of 15 July, a transcript of which is appended to this study, q.v. Appendix I.

[16] Loftus to Burghley, S. P. for I. 1 July 1592.

17 September,[17] we have a statement of the articles objected against the Lord Chancellor by the two spies, with joint answers by Loftus and Meath.

The Lord Chancellor was called on to explain: (1) a deficit of Crown forfeitures to the amount of £24,000; (2) the freeing from Dublin Castle of Connor O'Devana, a Romish bishop; (3) the holding of pleas of debts, Crown land and tithes in the Chancery court, contrary to the laws of the realm; (4) the use of maintenance in a case of the Bishop of Meath for certain tythes grown by Michael Fittsymons, a prisoner for treason; (5) maintaining Feagh Hugh O'Byrne in his disorders, Loftus' children having been fostered [18] in O'Byrne's country; (6) being touched with corruption and bribery for causes before him as Chancellor; (7) for disposing the livings of St. Patricks upon his kinsfolk and alliance, and later taking them in farm, and in keeping the Chancellorship of St. Patricks *in commendam* to himself.

These charges have been listed in full as illustrative of the opportunities which church preferment in Ireland presented to Anglican appointees. To each charge Loftus and Meath returned plausible replies or flat denials. However true or untrue the accusations may have been is impossible to say, for no action was taken by the government, and the two powerful brethren continued to flourish. It is certain that Loftus had an evil reputation in his own day and that he betrothed some of his children at very early ages to the most influential Irishmen of the realm, thus consolidating his power in Ireland by wide family connection.[19] Concerning Bishop Jones, sometime Dean of St. Patricks, evidence is more definite. "One extant deed,"

[17] Public Record Office, *Calendars of S. P. relating to I.* 17 Sept. 1592.

[18] "Fosterage" was the custom of lodging one's children in another man's household for education and training. When practised between English and Irish it cemented, naturally, a very intimate family relation and was therefore among the usages expressly forbidden by the Statutes of Kilkenny.

[19] Rych to the Privy Council, v. Appendix I.

writes Bagwell,[20] "bears Swift's indignant endorsement
made in 1714 as 'a lease of Coolmine made by that rascal
Dean Jones, and the knaves, or fools, his chapter, to one
John Allen for eighty one years made in 1583; so that
there was a lease for 161 years of 253 acres in Tassagard
parish, within three miles of Dublin for 2£ per annum
. . . now worth 150£, and so near Dublin, could not then
be worth less than 50£.'" Jones has a collateral, if indefi-
nite, literary interest in connection with the existence of
drama in Ireland. In a letter from his enemy Sir Richard
Bingham to Walsingham (24 June 1589) he is referred to
as so busy preparing a case against him (Bingham) that he
found no time to preach once during the three months
he spent at Galway, though "he would go to church in
the morning to hear an exercise and again in the afternoon
to hear a play." [21]

Once the identities of the informers were known, life,
for Rych at least, became a constant peril. The Lord Chancellor's men went out of their way to draw him into quarrels until, finally, he crossed again into England. There he
lay before the queen still another book of "informations,"
in return for which she made him her "sworn man," and
he returned to Ireland in the hope that this evidence of
favor would shield him from further quarrels.[22]

But the news of his book had gone before him, and the
Lord Chancellor and his brother and their following in-
ferred that other charges had been laid against them.
Shortly thereafter, a ruffian named Walsh, in company
with others of the Lord Chancellor's men, drew Rych into
a street brawl, but were worsted. The next day six others
lay in wait for him with drawn swords, if we are to credit
his own sensational account, and he barely escaped with his
life.[23] After the second attack and a futile petition to the

[20] Bagwell, III, 133.
[21] *Ibid.*, III, 211–212.
[22] Rych to the Privy Council, v. Appendix I.
[23] Appendix I.

Lord Chancellor for the peace of his men, Rych, under armed escort, took ship for England where he remained until 1598, by which time the ire of the Lord Chancellor had cooled. So ended Barnabe Rych's most notable exploit in the gathering of information for the service of his prince, though his personal and literary association with the Kingdom seems to have been almost continuous from his first crossing in 1573 to the end of his life.

# VII

## The Second Earl of Essex
## and
## Hugh Roe O'Neill of Tyrone

### 1594–1599

THE rebellion of Hugh Roe O'Neill, second Earl of Tyrone, like the Desmond rebellions before it, was linked with the inevitable Continental intrigue. As early as 1594 Hugh Roe, who in 1593 had succeeded to the leadership of his house, had embarked upon the usual course of Irish diplomacy by entering into negotiations with Spain. Meanwhile he had incurred the deadly enmity of Sir Henry Bagnal by eloping with that official's sister. Having raided the English Pale in 1595, no one was very surprised when in 1597, after two years of temporizing, he saw fit to call a general "rising out." [1] Bagnal at once marched against him, but was himself killed and his army routed by Hugh Roe at the Yellow Ford on the River Curran. O'Neill now forced the evacuation of the English Fort at Blackwater and, moving westward, played havoc with the new plantations.

Fired by the example of Tyrone, the southern Irish sprang to arms and ravaged plantation and manor with torch and sword. Mutilated English fugitives flocked to the walled garrison towns. Spenser fled from Kilcolman; Raleigh's seignory was laid waste, the castle of Sir Warham St. Leger destroyed. Irish raiders pillaged the estates of Sir Thomas Norris. [2] At Enniscorthy the Irish put to the sword over a hundred household retainers of Sir Henry Wallopp,

---

[1] Bagwell, III, 273.
[2] *Ibid.*, III, 304–305.

and Wallopp's protégé, Lodowick Bryskett, with his family and what goods he was able, fled to Waterford and so, like Spenser and many another refugee, to England. Thus, out of the number of friends to whom Bryskett played host at his cottage near Dublin, the only two not definitely known to have suffered at the hands of Tyrone allies are Master Smith the apothecary, and the Archbishop of Ardmagh.

In 1599 the much harassed viceroy, Thomas Lord Burgh, was recalled to England, and Robert Devereux, the second Earl of Essex, was sent to Ireland as Lord Lieutenant to "bring home rebellion broached on his sword." [3] Essex, having received express instructions to break the power of Tyrone, sailed from England with virtually unlimited powers, and a splendid army of twenty thousand veterans. With the Essex expedition sailed four young officers who were also ready on occasion with the pen, Captain Josias Bodley, Gervase Markham, Robert Prickett, and John Harington.

## JOSIAS BODLEY
### 1550?–1618

Josias Bodley, soldier and military engineer and brother of Sir Thomas the collector, was the fifth and youngest son of John Bodley of Exeter. Not much is known of his early life [4] beyond Anthony Wood's statement that he had been a member of Merton College, Oxford. After military service in the Netherlands, Bodley came to Ireland in 1598 with troops drawn from Holland to take the field against Tyrone, and he served successively under Burgh, Essex, and Mountjoy. Among numerous references to Bodley in Fynes Moryson's *Itinerary*, the following is of especial interest as illustrating the method of attack upon an Irish crannoge or island stronghold:

[3] Bagwell, III, 313 ff.
[4] C. L. Falkiner, *Illustrations of Irish History*, London, 1904. v. biog. note.

The sixth of April 1601, his Lordship received advertisement from Captain Josias Bodley, at the Newry, that he, and Captain Edward Blany, Governor of the Fort of Mount-Norris, purposing to surprise Loghrorcan, could not carry a boat, which they had provided to that purpose, but he carrying certain fireworks provided in case the boat should fail, went to the Fort, and joining with Captain Blany, marched towards that Island, where they arrived by eight of the clock in the morning, and leaving their forces behind in a Wood, they both went together to discover the Island; which done Captain Bodley made ready thirty arrows with wildfire, and so they both fell down with one hundred shot close to the water, where the shot playing incessantly upon the Island, while the other delivered their arrows, suddenly at the houses fired, and burnt so vehemently, as the rebels lodging there, forsook the Island, and swum to the further shore. That after they saw all burnt to the ground, they fired a great house upon their side of the shore, and killed there six Kern, (gaining their Arms) beside Churls and Calliachs (old women), and after the burning of other houses also, they brought away some cows and sheep, with other pillage; and they understood by a prisoner, that there were about thirty persons in the Island, whereof only eight swum away, (of which four were shot in the water), so as the rest either were killed or lay hurt in the Island. Likewise they understood by the said prisoner, that great store of butter, corn, meal, and powder, was burnt and spoiled in the Island, which all the rebels of that Country made their magazine.[5]

In the same year (November 1601), while Governor of Newry, Bodley undertook the journey celebrated in his delightful essay, a rollicking and vivid account of the English official in his Irish country house. The *Descriptio* (*lepida*) *itineris d. Iosiae Bodleii ad Lecaliam in Ultonia anno* 1602,[6] has, if anything, gained in freshness by its Latin brine. Turbulent, patched out with English where the Latin wears thin, it loses nothing by translation except the archaism of Elizabethan phrase. Color of thought, rich humor, and a workaday philosophy of life, love, and drink—such are the qualities of the bluff soldier in that age or this.

In December Bodley and two fellow officers, Captain Caulfeild and Captain Jephson, all of whom were then in

[5] Moryson, *Itinerary*, II, 372–373.
[6] Falkiner, *Illustrations of Irish History*, ed. and tr. *Journey to Lecale*, VII, 385 ff.

garrison at Carrickfergus with the forces of Chichester, received letters from Sir Richard Moryson, Governor of Downpatrick, inviting them to keep Christmas with him in his house at Lecale.

It was not until after Christmas that they were able to get leave, but, deciding that their welcome would be equally warm for New Year's, the Pickwickian party set out with no guide but Caulfeild, who promptly led them astray in the bogs and marshes. Coming at length to a village, for "two brass shillings" they hired a guide to take them to the island of Maginnis where Moryson met them and squired them the rest of the way:

When we had approached within a stone's throw of the house, or rather palace, of the said Master Moryson—behold! forthwith innumerable servants! Some light us with pinewood lights and torches, because it is dark; others, as soon as we alight, take our horses and lead them into a handsome and spacious stable, where neither hay nor oats are wanting. Master Moryson himself leads us by wide stairs into a large hall, where a fire is burning the height of our chins, as the saying is, and afterwards into a bed-chamber prepared in the Irish fashion.

Here, having taken off our boots, we all sit down and converse on various matters: Captain Caulfeild about supper and food, for he was very hungry; Captain Constable about hounds, of which he had there some excellent ones, as he himself asserted; and the rest about other things. Master Moryson ordered a cup of Spanish wine to be brought, with burnt sugar, nutmeg and ginger, and made us all drink a good draught of it, which was very grateful to the palate, and also good for procuring an appetite for supper if anyone needed such. . . .

In an hour we heard someone down in the kitchen calling with a loud voice "to the dresser." Forthwith we see a long row of servants decently dressed, each with dishes of the most select meats, which they place on the table in the very best style. One presents to us a silver basin with the most limpid water, another hands us a very white towel, others arrange chairs and seats in their proper places.

*Denique quid verbis opus est? spectemus agendo*

(As Ajax says in Ovid). Grace having been said, we begin to fix our eyes intently on the dishes whilst handling our knives; and here you might have plainly seen those Belgian feasts where,

*In principio est silentium,*
*In medio stridor dentium,*
*Et in fine rumor gentium.*

For at first we sat as if rapt and astounded by the variety of meats and dainties—like a German I once saw depicted standing between two jars, the one of white wine, the other of claret, with this motto: "I know not which way to turn."

A jovial excursion into the pleasures of the table and enumeration and eulogy suggestive of Martial's gustatory epigrams ends with:

. . . supper . . . being ended, we again enter our bedroom, in which was a large fire (for at that time it was exceedingly cold out of doors) and benches for sitting on, and plenty of tobacco, with nice pipes, was set before us. The wine also had begun to operate a little on us, and everyone's wits had become somewhat sharper; all were gabbling at once, like what Sir Roger Williams of worthy memory used to call "his academy" to wit, where all were speakers and no listeners. And it is not true that some say "When wine is in wit is out" unless they mean thereby that when anyone is full of wine, then his wit, that was previously hidden and unknown, exhibits itself openly and plainly. For if any sober person had been present at that time in any corner of the room, I doubt not but that he would have heard many remarkable and witty things which I cannot now recollect.

Chatty comments follow touching on arrangements for the night: how their host took a hard pallet for himself and gave his featherbed to them; how Captain Constable's hounds crept in with them for warmth, and how the dogs howled and Constable swore when they kicked them out in the cold; how they were waked for a morning collation of usquebaugh and tobacco.

That night they were visited by masquers, an interesting example of a custom then apparently in use among the native Irish gentry to disguise themselves for a gaming match. They entered,

. . . first a boy with lighted torch; then two beating drums; then the maskers two and two; then another torch. One of the maskers carried a dirty pocket-handkerchief with ten pounds in it, not of bullion but of the new money lately coined which has the harp on one side and the royal arms on the other. They were dressed in shirts with many ivy leaves sewn on here and there over them, and had over their faces masks of dog-skin with holes to see out of, and noses made of paper; their caps were high and peaked (in the Persian fashion) and were also of paper and ornamented with the same leaves.

The company then played at dice until the visitors, stripped of their money, departed in chagrin. The host then called two of his servants in to entertain the guests by a passage at "skivar (skewer) -the-goose." This curious Hibernian pastime Bodley describes as follows:

The contestants sat down upon the floor face to face with the space of an ell between them. Each doubled forward from the waist till the angle of his elbows overlapped the angle of his knees. Elbows and knees were now locked together by a short wooden bar. After this, seconds tied together each man's wrists, thrust into his bound hands a sharp stick or skewer, and gave the sign for combat. The object of each hero was then, by kicking with his feet, to roll the other helplessly back on his buttocks, and with the sharpened stick to "skivar the goose." "Which made us laugh so for an hour," ends Bodley, "that the tears dropped from our eyes."

With the Journey to *Lecale*, Bodley's whimsical excursion into letters begins and ends. Serving with distinction at Kinsale and Waterford under Mountjoy, Bodley was knighted in 1604, and variously employed in military engineering until 1609, when commissioned to survey the Ulster Plantation. In recognition of this work, he received by letters patent (3 December 1612) the appointment as Director General of the Fortifications in Ireland for life. He died 19 August 1617.

The relation of Markham and Prickett to this study is less organic, though both were associated with Essex and in his service during the period of his ill-advised and feeble efforts against Tyrone.

## GERVASE MARKHAM
### 1568?–1637

Gervase Markham, known to literature as a general
pamphleteer, after seeking fortune in the European battle
ground of the Low Countries, followed Essex into Ireland
and served under his command in company with his
brother Francis and his cousin, Sir Griffin Markham.[7]
Though specific Irish themes appear in none of his books
on farriery and sport, his work is the best contemporary
source for the conduct of field amusements current among
the English both at home and abroad in Ireland. Irish
hunters, hawks, and hounds were held in high estimation,[8]
not only in England but throughout continental Europe,
and it is on such subjects that Markham was a recognized
authority in his age. Few phases of husbandry or what we
now name generically "domestic science" escaped his indefatigable pen, and his writings in the department of sport
constitute a Tudor analogue to the present undertakings
of Badminton or Spalding. Equestrianism, archery, dog-
breeding, hawking, hunting, fishing, cockfighting, and "all
recreations meet for a gentleman" are themes for Markham, and are dealt with in a delightful expository style. He
appears at his quaint best in the *Art of Archery* (1634),
a book of instruction embodying a suggestion that the re-
vival of the art will relieve the "half-lost Societies of
Bowyers and Fletchers," and provide a reserve of bow-
and-arrow minute-men useful to have on call should a national emergency arise. Equally interesting is his essay on
the breeding and handling of gamecocks in his *Way to
Get Wealth* (1631). Pleasant touches of the artless esoteric
crop up here and there, as, *The Several Wayes . . . for the
Destruction of Moals, or Moles which digg and root up the*

[7] *D. N. B.*
[8] Moryson, IV, 194.

*Earth.* After a practical description of how to use the mole-spear or to flood the ground, he writes:

A third affirms. That if you take green Leeks, Garlick or Onions, and choping them grosly, thrust it into the holes, the very fume or savor thereof will so astonish and amaze the Moale, that they will presently forsake the Earth, and falling into a Trance, you may take them up with your hands.[9]

In addition to his handbooks relating to the useful arts, Markham tried his hand at devotional verse, and collaborated in two plays, *The Dumb Knight* (1608) and *The True Tragedy of Herod and Antipater* (1622).

## ROBERT PRICKETT

### fl. 1603–1645

Concerning the life of Robert Prickett, almost nothing is known beyond the fact that he was a soldier by profession, and that he saw service with, and presumably under, Essex whom he admired deeply. He is interesting in his prose tracts, however, as an exemplar of the Protestant virulence against the Pope and the Roman Catholic faith characteristic of the soldier-pamphleteer of his age. Both Rych and Churchyard shared that violence, and many another like them who, schooled to War in the Low Countries, had come to identify with Catholicism such cruelties as that described by Gascoigne who, from a vantage point in a church tower in Antwerp, saw the Duke of Alva's soldiers cast seven thousand Protestant wounded upon a great fire to cook in their armor.[10]

The work for which Prickett is chiefly remembered is his elegy to the memory of Essex, *Honor's Fame in Triumph Riding* (1604). The closing stanza of this effort of Prick-

[9] *Inrichment of the Weald of Kent*, 1683, p. 71.

[10] (British Museum 115 A 17) *The Spoyle of Antwerpe. Faithfully reported by a true Englishman who was present at the same Novem. 1576* . . . (8° A-Ci. Attributed to George Gascoigne.)

ett's pedestrian Muse discloses alike his devotion and his tastelessness:

> Base wretch, whose hand true honors blood should spill,
>     death's axe did first into his shoulder strike;
> Upreard againe he strikes a blow as ill
>     nor one nor other were directed right.
> Honor ne'er moov'd, a third blow did devide
> The body from the worlds admired pride:
>         Was that the way to lose a head,
>         To have an Earle so butchered?

## SIR JOHN HARINGTON

### 1561–1612

In Sir John Harington, translator, critic, epigrammatist, courtier, and godson to the Queen, who sailed to Ireland with Essex in 1599, we have an interesting link with names familiar to us from the earlier pages of this study. Harington was educated at Eton and Cambridge and read law for a short time at Lincoln's Inn. He came into his patrimony in 1582 and thenceforward applied himself to the court. That he knew Ireland as early as 1586 we know from his allusion to having tarried there, in connection, says his editor, N. E. McClure, with undertaking attainted Desmond lands in Munster.[11] Crossing to Ireland as captain of horse under Southampton, he was one of the officers knighted by Essex. We learn from one of his letters that he served at the Curlews with Captain Jephson—the same Jephson who made one of Josias Bodley's party at Lecale. In another place he speaks of the brothers Gervase and Francis Markham as related to him through their father, Robert Markham of Cottam, Nottinghamshire, and of having received courtesies at their hands. Elsewhere he alludes to the Queen's displeasure incurred through a suspicion of

---

[11] N. E. McClure, *Sir John Harington*, Introduction.

complicity with Essex, a result, it may be, of having gone with Sir William Warren in October, 1599, to treat with the Earl of Tyrone. But more interesting still for the purposes of this study is the circumstance that the tract which relates him to Ireland—*A View of the State of Ireland in 1605*—is in substance an application for appointment to two offices then held by that arch-enemy to Barnabe Rych, Adam Loftus, who lay on his deathbed at the time of its writing. The MS, dated 20 April 1605, was addressed to Christopher Blount, late Lord Lieutenant of Ireland, and its tone is very similar to that of the letters written in 1581 by Bryskett who, as we have seen, solicited the Lord Grey's influence to get him the appointment as Secretary of Ireland held at the time by the dying Sir John Challoner. It will be recalled that Bryskett was unsuccessful. Harington's case was no better, for the See of Dublin and the Chancellery of Privy Seal went to Thomas Jones, Bishop of Meath.

The *View of Ireland* is valuable as an example of the liberal Tudor point of view; it offers nothing in the way of graphic record. It does, however, state with clarity the view of that rare Englishman able to divine as between Saxon and Celt a common ground of human reasonableness, and liberal enough to deprecate the policy of Church and Army alike which in its extremes of severity defeated its own ends. As an advocate of logic and of compromise, therefore, Harington urged his executive fitness to King James' Council:

Whear I saw Crosses or Images remayning in any of theyr Churches or howses (he writes), I told them owr Church did not condemne the use but the abuse of these, when throwgh a neglygent and affected ygnoraunce the people creep to them and are prostrate afore them as to deytyes; but for those that wold breake them and defase them . . . I asswerd them owr Church held them as worthy of punishment as owr State held theyr cowntrymen that trayld Queen Elizabeth's picture at his horse tayle.

Harington goes on to point out the fallacy of trying to suppress by arbitrary means the Roman Catholic forms of worship; he urges as having the greater efficacy a policy of reasoned mildness and of conciliation. He tells how, in his relations with the Irish, his effort is to explain at every opportunity that the offices read in Latin by the Catholic priests differ no whit in essence and spirit from those read in English by the Anglican clergy. He explains how he tries to show them that apostolic succession is as equally the right of every bishop as it is of the pope. In a word, his effort is to reconcile points of conflicting dogma by showing it is only a difference of form that veils an identity of devotional spirit:

> By these & such kynd of mild conferences many may bee wonne, and not as owr men have caused them by vyolent hewing down theyr crosses, burning and defasing theyr ymages, rayling in the pulpet on all theyr Saynts and ceremonyes, feasting on Ash-wednesdays and Good-Frydays, going to plow on theyr Christmas-days, and pronowncing that all theyr awncestors are damned that did but pray to owr Lady, with soch lyke, as yt ys no marvell yf soch laborers have in 44 yeers made so slender an harvest.

Harington closes his argument with the inevitable buttress of prose writers of his age—a scroll of precedents to show how in the past courtiers and wits like himself have, after a sobering experience, turned successful hands to the administration of the highest offices of Church and State. He affirms that he has now reached a mood of grave reflectiveness, and assures the Lords Councillors that to poetry and all light studies he has bidden a long farewell.

In addition to the *View of Ireland,* Harington wrote a journal covering his Irish experience with Essex which, he tells us, he read to the Queen as one of the conditions of his restoration to her favor. In the opinion of the editor of the *View,* W. D. Macray, this journal has been incorporated verbatim in the *Treatise of Ireland* of John Dymock, an historian and annalist who belongs to the same period.

Of Harington's letters from Ireland, all dated 1599, the first describes the fight at Curlews and the Pare. The second contains data relating to the pay and appareling of English soldiery in the Irish service. In the last and most interesting, Harington tells how he went with Sir William Warren to treat with the Earl of Tyrone, and describes the pleasure of the Earl at Harington's gift of his English translation of Ariosto to his sons.

John Harington seems to have had neither the force nor the experience needed for success in Ireland, and it is in every way likely that the moderation we admire in him now would have been his undoing in the offices he so vainly sought. Nor can we express surprise that his seeking was vain. What wonder the Council smiled when, even as one's attention follows the arguments of his eager bid for Irish service, an errant, retrospective whim recalls his epigram entitled *Of the Warres in Ireland,* whose closing lines are these:

> Lo then how greatly their opinions erre,
> That thinke there is no great delight in warre:
> But yet for this (sweet warre) Ile be thy debtor,
> I shall forever love my home the better.

# VIII

# *Consolidation of English Power by Mountjoy and Chichester*

## 1599–1608

THE vigorous Lord Mountjoy succeeded incapable Essex with an army of thirteen thousand men. With him from England came Sir George Carew with the title of Lord President of Munster. Sending a detachment to take Ulster from the Connaught border, Mountjoy advanced with his main body toward the Blackwater, laying waste the country as he passed, and fortifying the passes through the woods. By the spring of 1601 he had firmly established himself at Ardmagh, and held several other strategic points in the rebels' country.

A few months earlier Sir Richard Moryson, the same whose hospitality Bodley had celebrated in the *Journey to Lecale,* seems to have sent his brother, Fynes Moryson, the traveler and historian, an invitation to come over to Ireland,[1] the possibility of a secretaryship to the Lord Deputy being in the wind.

## FYNES MORYSON

### 1566–1630

On 13 November, Fynes Moryson reached Dundalk, where Sir Richard was then Governor, and the same day the Lord Deputy's chief secretary, Charles Cranmer, was killed at Carlingford. Moryson was at once appointed to his place. Thus the younger brother of Sir George, an experienced traveler and indefatigable diarist, found him-

---

[1] Moryson, *Itinerary,* II, 341.

self in the close confidence of Sir Charles Blount from the time when O'Neill's power was at its summit to the rout at Kinsale. He accompanied the Lord Deputy everywhere, and the official files were at his disposal. The result was a vivid and refreshingly uncritical history of the Tyrone rebellion in the form of a journal covering the period 1599 on till 1603 when Moryson returned with Mountjoy to England where, receiving a Crown pension in 1604, he saw through the press the greater part of his travel journal, the *Itinerary* . . . (1606). Seven years later, in the autumn of 1613, Moryson revisited Ireland at the invitation of his brother, then Vice-President of Munster, and has left an interesting opinion of the country as he found it.

There is hardly a phase of Tudor Irish life that Moryson does not touch on, from the least to the greatest. The length of the Irish mile, the currency, Irish nature, topography, minerals, flora and fauna, food and travel—all have mention in one place or another; but Moryson is at his best when dealing with his own feelings and experiences in the field and by the Lord Deputy at the council table, or billeted in the uncleanly Irish houses which he pictures with such graphic disrelish.

Moryson's account of the wild Irish at home affords an interesting contrast to Bodley's domestic idyl of Captain Richard Moryson's house at Lecale.

These wild Irish never set any candles upon tables; What do I speak of Tables? since indeed they have no tables, but set their meat upon a bundle of grass, and use the same Grass for napkins to wipe their hands. But I mean that they do not set candles upon any high place to give light to the house, but place a great candle made of reeds and butter upon the floor in the midst of a great room. And in like sort the chief men in their houses make fires in the midst of the room, the smoke whereof goeth out at a hole in the top thereof. . . . I trust no man expects among these gallants any beds, much less featherbeds and sheets, who like the Nomads removing their dwellings, according to the commodity of pastures for their Cows, sleep under the canopy of heaven, or in a poor house of clay, or in a cabin made of the boughs of trees, and covered with turf, for such are the dwellings of the very Lords among them. And in such places, they make a fire in the midst of the room, and round about it they sleep upon the ground, without straw or other thing under them, lying all in a circle about the fire, with their feet towards it. And their bodies being naked, they cover their heads and upper parts with their mantles, which they first make very wet, steeping them in water of purpose, for they find that when their bodies have once warmed the wet mantles, the smoke of them keeps their bodies in temperate heat all the night following. And this manner of lodging, not only the mere Irish Lords and their followers use, but even some of the English Irish Lords and their followers, when after the old but tyrannical and prohibited manner vulgarly called Coshering, they go (as it were) on progress, to live upon their tenants, till they have consumed all the victuals that the poor men have or can get.[2]

In diet, according to Moryson, the wild Irishman is barbarous and filthy, straining cow's milk through dirty straw and boiling beef or pork together with the entrails in a raw cowhide for want of a pot, swallowing it with "whole lumps of filthy butter." The dearness of usquebaugh as a beverage to the hearts of the Tudor Irish ought to be fairly clear from its literal Gaelic meaning—water of life. The woodcut that faces this page gives a burlesque portraiture of an Irish feast. We note in passing that harpers and bards had the privilege of taking meat from the dish of the chief. Not to be omitted from any discussion of the northern Irish is a passage from the *Total Discourse* of William Lithgow the traveler who, writing somewhat later, observes that he saw in Ireland's Northern parts two remarkable sights:

. . . The one was their manner of Tillage, Ploughes drawne by Horsetayles, wanting garnishing, Ropes to their bare Rumps, marching all side for side, three or four in a Ranke, and as many men hanging by the ends of that untoward labour. . . .

The other as goodly sight I saw, was women travayling the way, or toyling at home, carry their Infants about their neckes, and laying

[2] Moryson, *Itinerary*, IV, 202–203.

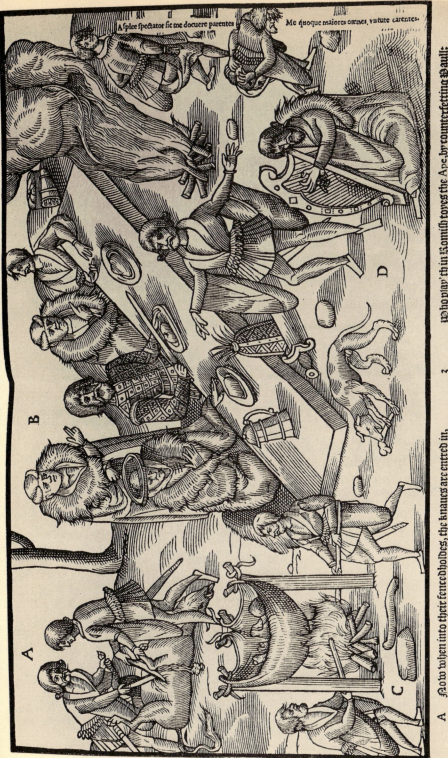

Aspice spectator sic me docuere parentes    Me quoque maiores omnes, virtute carentes.

A  Now when into their fenced holdes, the knaues are entred in,
   To smite and knocke the cateil downe, the hangmen doe beginne.
   One plucketh off the Oxes cote, which be euen now did weare:
   Another lacking pannes, to boyle the flesh, his hide doe prepare.
C  These theeues attend vpon the fire, for seruing vp the feast:
B  And Fryer smelfeast sneaking in, doth preace amongst the best.

3  Who play' thin Romish toyes the Ape, by counterfetting Paull:
   For which they doe aboard him then, the highest roome of all.
   Who being set, because the cheere, is deemd litle worth:
   Except the same be intermixt, and larde with Irish myrth.
D  Both Barde, and Harper, is prepard, which by their cunning art,
   Doe strike and cheare vp all the gests, with comfort at the hart.

the dugges over their shoulders, would give sucke to the Babes behind their backes, without taking them in their armes.[3]

Irish men and women who lived among the English followed English fashions in dress, but in remoter districts, it is affirmed that both sexes went practically naked in summer, in winter wearing only shoes and the Irish mantle, a triangular garment with a hood of fur. Waterford was famed for the weaving of the mantle, the shaggy appearance of which is illustrated by Stanihurst's story of a friend of his who, being in London and the morning frosty, went to the Paris garden wrapped in a Waterford rug. The mastiffs at once sprang at him, "deeming he had been a beare." [4]

Yet Moryson's vignettes of social life in Ireland, vivid as they are, are incidental to his main intention, the history of the Tyrone rebellion of 1598–1603, and the panegyric of that rebellion's English hero, Charles Blount, Lord Mountjoy.

*The Rebellion of Hugh Earl of Tyrone* is at once the most elaborate and most authoritative Tudor account of the Tyrone rebellion, and as such deserves a brief analysis. Here Moryson shows to best advantage in dealing with palpable facts and impressions. A good subordinate and a faithful partisan, he is untrammeled by soul searchings as to the possible humanity of the Irish race; his bias is simple, clear, and naïf.

The causes of the rebellion, he tells us, were five: the shiring of Ulster and the planting of garrison towns in county Tyrone, the difference of religion, the extortion of sheriffs and sub-sheriffs, and the disaffection fostered by popish priests.[5]

Tyrone's estrangement from fealty to the Crown seems

[3] Sir J. Froissart, *Chronicles of England, France and Spain*. Ed. T. Jonnes, New York (n.d.), pp. 569 f.

[4] Stanihurst in *Holinshed*, VI, 29.

[5] Moryson, *Itinerary*, II, 190.

to have begun in 1594, and Moryson traces with great skill the course of his temporizing during the next few years while awaiting ordinance and soldiers from Spain. As a sometime commander in the royal forces, O'Neill understood the necessity of opposing trained band to trained band; to that end he hit upon a clever scheme of contriving that the Queen train and arm his soldiers for him.[6] Taking advantage of the notorious army abuse and malfeasance in the invaders' armies, abuses such as those satirized by Shakespeare in the second part of *Henry IV*, he sent Irishmen to volunteer for service in the English bands for lower than the regular pay or for no pay at all. Captains of such bands were glad to accept these volunteers and pocket the difference between what the regular soldier demanded and the Irishman's cut-rate pittance. Ulster loyalists thus received both training and equipment from the Queen, but when called upon to serve against their tribal lords, promptly went "over the hill" and joined the enemy camp.[7] By this and other equally ingenious shifts, and owing not a little to material aid from the Spanish, O'Neill by 1598 had at his command the most formidable power ever to oppose the English on Irish ground.

The outbreak of hostilities began with the arrival of three thousand English veterans from Brittany for garrison duty at Ballyshannon and Relike, both in Tyrone country. The fort at Blackwater fell. O'Neill then sued for pardon while soliciting help from Spain. Delays wore on for two years, a time of desultory skirmishes followed by complaints and extenuations to the Lord Deputy or the Queen. Lord Burgh died in 1597, and Sir Thomas Norris succeeded him for a short month's tenure as Lord Lieutenant of the Kingdom. Norris was succeeded by Adam Loftus, Lord Chancellor of Ireland and Lord Archbishop of Dub-

---

[6] Moryson, *Itinerary*, II, 192; Rych, *Anothomy of Ireland.* v. Appendix III.
[7] Appendix III.

lin, holding office jointly with Robert Gardiner, Chief
Justice of Ireland for the civil government, while the Earl
of Ormonde served as Lord Lieutenant of the army. On the
22 December 1597, Ormonde and Geoffrey Fenton met
O'Neill at Dundalk,[8] and a truce was signed and articles
of pardon agreed to.

Early in 1598 the pardon was confirmed, only to be
violated by an immediate attack at Blackwater. Sir Henry
Bagnal, sent with an army of four thousand to the relief
of the fort, was killed with half his army. "All Ulster was
in Arms," writes Moryson, "all Connaught revolted, and
the rebels of Leinster swarmed in the English Pale, while
the English lay in their Garrisons, so far from assailing the
Rebels, as they rather lived in continual fear to be surprised
by them." [9]

In this year Essex, even then preparing to take command
in Ireland, had sent into Leinster under the command of
Sir Samuel Bagnal two thousand veterans officered, among
others, by the heroes of the *Journey to Lecale,* Josias Bodley, John Jephson, Toby Caulfeild, and Edward Blany.
About the same time the rebellion spread into Munster, at a
fearful cost to the English "undertakers" there. Moryson's
comment is brief and unsympathetic.

And to speak truth, Munster undertakers . . . were in great part,
cause of this defection, and of their own fatal miseries. For whereas they
should have built Castles, and brought over Colonies of English, and
have admitted no Irish Tenant, but only English, these and like cove-
nants were in no part performed by them. Of whom the men of best
quality never came over, but made profit of the land; others brought
no more English than their own Families, and all entertained Irish servants and tenants, which were now the first to betray them.[10]

The veterans, landing before Essex' arrival, were dis-
persed into the regiments of new men "to season them and

[8] Moryson, *Itinerary,* II, 220.
[9] *Ibid.,* II, 217.
[10] *Ibid.,* II, 219.

replenish them with sufficient officers." A relation of Essex'
futile marches follows, a vivid vignette of the Earl's meeting with O'Neill at the ford of Ballaclinch in County
Louth,[11] and his sudden departure in 1599, the year of the
death of Sir Thomas Norris. Moryson mentions by the way
the rumor attributed to O'Neill, "that England would
shortly be in combustion within itself, which increased the
suspicions already conceived of the foresaid conference had
between the Earl and Tyrone, to the great prejudice of the
Earl being in durance." [12]

Of Mountjoy, Moryson has left the following vivid
"character":

He was of stature tall, and of very comely proportion, his skin fair,
with little hair on his body, which hair was of color blackish (or in-
clining to black), and thin on his head . . . His forehead was broad
and high; his eyes great, black, and lovely; his nose something low
and short, and a little blunt in the end; his chin round; his cheeks
full, round, and ruddy; his countenance cheerful, and as amiable as
ever I beheld of any man. . . . His arms were long and of proportion-
able bigness, his hands long and white, his fingers great in the end, and
his legs somewhat little, which he gartered ever above the knee, wearing the Garter of St. Georges order under the left knee, except when he
was booted, and so wore not that Garter, but a blue ribbon in stead
thereof above his knee, and hanging over his boot.[13]

Nowhere better than here in his portrait of his patron
and hero is there better illustration of Moryson's exact
painstaking objectivity. It gives one the confidence that
elsewhere, as here, he saw the world about him literally, and
literally recorded it.

Moryson now carries us through the Tyrone campaign
to Kinsale, quoting by the way important documents of
state, and giving army and civil lists in which many familiar names are met with, among them his own, Rych, Legg,
Caulfeild, Fenton, Raleigh, and Spenser. He gives a spirited

[11] Moryson, *Itinerary*, II, 219.
[12] *Ibid.*
[13] *Ibid.*, II, 261.

account of the coming of six thousand Spaniards under Don Juan D'Aguila and of the siege of Kinsale in Cork, where Bodley served as trenchmaster, and of the victory of the Lord Deputy and Sir George Carew.[14]

The back of the rebellion thus broken, Mountjoy went systematically about the final subjugation of the kingdom. He quartered garrisons at strategic points throughout the island. He then took the field with a small, highly mobile force, subject always to reinforcement from the nearest strong point in the event of a major action.[15] The great army which Essex had been the means of bringing into Ireland, and which he knew not how to employ, was strengthened, disciplined, and rendered effective by the generalship of Mountjoy, and employed to its greatest tactical advantage, so that by 1603, the year of his return to England—and Moryson's—the work of military sub-jugation was done. What remained to do, for two decades at least, was the task of civil administration.

The spokesman of the civil council table, as Moryson had been for the field, was Sir John Davies, author of *Nosce Teipsum*, who had been appointed Attorney-General for Ireland in 1603 by James I.

## SIR JOHN DAVIES

### 1569–1626

Sir John Davies took his degree at Queen's College, Oxford, in 1590, went down to London, and after a short and stormy residence at the Inns of Court, resumed residence at the University in 1599 where he devoted himself to poetry and reflection. One of the results of this period was the poem by which he is chiefly known, *Nosce Teipsum*, which, dedicated to Elizabeth at the suggestion of Davies' friend, Charles Blount, Lord Mountjoy, then Lord

[14] *Ibid.*, III, 15.
[15] *Ibid.*, II, 270.

Deputy in Ireland, opened the way to preferment. In 1601 he was readmitted to the Middle Temple and, entering politics, was returned to Parliament as member for Corfe Castle.[16]

When James I came to the throne in 1603, Davies' reputation as a philosophic poet again served him well. Through the good offices of Lord Hunsdon and Lord Mountjoy, he was called to Ireland as Attorney-General, and there continued till 1616, successively enjoying the honorable offices of King's Sergeant, Member for Fermanagh in the Parliament of 1613, and Speaker of the House. To modern historians with Irish sympathies, a dark aura invests Davies' memory by reason of a decision rendered in 1607 which voided the freehold rights of the tenants of the departed earls of Tyrone and Tyrconnel whose lands had been attainted.[17] In justice to Davies let it be said that the entire body of his prose writings relating to Ireland is a deeply sincere assertion of his belief that absolute English dominion in Ireland was all for the ultimate Irish weal.

Davies' *Discovery of the true causes why Ireland was never entirely subdued* (1612) [18] shows a power of analysis, historic perspective, and political insight suggestive at times of his contemporary, Francis Bacon. He is not content with facts; he probes back to causes with the balanced incisiveness of a brilliant philosophic mind.

The reasons for the lawlessness of Ireland, he writes, are two: mismanagement of the army and inefficiency in the civil administration. Owing to the preoccupation of English kings with more urgent matters, the forces in Ireland have been either too weak for conquest, or when strong enough, too soon broken up, or ill disciplined or ill paid.

Want of regular pay led in the reign of King Edward II

---

[16] H. Morley, *Ireland Under Elizabeth and James*, v. prefatory sketch, pp. 27 f.
[17] *Ibid.*
[18] A. Grosart (ed.), *Prose Works of Sir John Davies*, London, 1876.

to billeting the soldiery upon the civil population, and elsewise loosing them upon the English colonists to take their dues as they would. This custom, called *coyne and livery,* practised with government sanction, gave the example to the great Anglo-Norman lords throughout the island, who similarly grazed their private retainers upon English freeholders settled within their seignories. Burdened past bearing, these English emigrated from Ireland, whereupon their erstwhile lords and patrons seized upon the freeholds thus left empty, and farmed them out to Irishmen from whom greater extortions might be wrung with less trouble. It did not take them long to discover how in addition to rent and *coyne and livery,* the Irish tenants could be made to yield *cosherings, cessings, cuttings,*[19] and other taxes sanctioned by march or brehon law. *Fosterage* and *gossipred* between English and Irish followed in natural course, and the English, being thus closely bound to their Irish neighbors by both material interest and personal ties, were soon weaned from political and racial allegiance to the Crown. "By this it appeareth," writes Davies, "why *coyne and livery* is called in the Old Statutes a damnable custom; and the imposing and taking thereof made high treason." [20]

The analysis given above should illustrate Davies' gift for cold thinking and close logic, especially when compared with the dry fact-stringing of the annalists, the disdain of Moryson, and the mordant bitterness of Spenser.

Proceeding from military to civil considerations, Davies scores as mistaken the policy that excluded Irishmen from the benefits of English law, and the vast extent of the early land grants which removed each proprietor beyond the horizon of direct official oversight. Preferential status and

[19] *Coshering,* food for chiefs and their following; *cessing,* billeting of soldiery; *cuttings,* taxes in money or in kind.
[20] Davies, *Discovery,* p. 45.

distance bred personal ambition at the cost of Crown authority.[21] Moreover, the adventurers in making their abode in the plains and open country, and driving the Irish to the woods and mountains, committed a fatal error, for the outlawed Irish grew wilder, "multiplied in infinite numbers, keeping their fastnesses secret and the entrances thereto impassable, stealing the cattle from which they lived." [22]

Here we have the first common-sense background sketch of the woodkern so detested of Derricke and Moryson, Stanihurst, Lithgow, and Hooker. It is not without meaning that Davies lays the responsibility for their wildness and estate squarely at the doorstep of the Anglo-Norman invaders. In characteristic analytic vein, Davies turns his attention to the custom of *gavelkind* and the reasons for clan and sept solidarity.

*Gavelkind,* or the custom of equal divisions of estate among all heirs male, both legal and bastard, made every heir a gentleman—a poor gentleman—too proud to work, but not too principled to steal. Thence large numbers of blooded idlers whose sole profession was war; thence too a sept and clan solidarity by blood alliance, very dangerous in time of rebellion. For these folk "rather choose to live at home by Theft, Extortion, and Coshering, than to seek any better fortunes abroad, which increased their Septs or Surnames in such numbers, as there are not to be found in any kingdom of Europe so many gentlemen of one Blood, Family, and Surname as there are of the O'Neills in Ulster, of the Burkes in Connaught; of the Geraldines and Butlers in Munster and Leinster." [23]

Finally, Davies traces the awakening of the Queen and her council to the threat of an Ireland dominated by the Roman Catholic powers of Italy and Spain; the extension

[21] Davies, *Discovery,* p. 83.
[22] *Ibid.,* pp. 98–99.
[23] *Ibid.,* p. 103.

of shire land in the firm administration of Sir Henry Sidney, John Perrot, and succeeding viceroys; and the happy success of Blount and Chichester in the opening decade of the new century.[24]

But now (1610), he writes, both the defects of the military and of the civil establishment have been mended: the military by good pay and strict discipline, the civil by the extension of English law to the suits of Irish plaintiffs, and by the new circuits for Justices of Assize which include the whole of Ireland which is now for the first time shire ground.[25]

. . . these civil assemblies at Assizes and Sessions, have reclaimed the Irish from their wildness, caused them to cut off their Glibs, and long Hair; to convert their Mantles into Cloaks, and conform themselves to the manner of England in all their behaviour and outward forms. . . . And because they find a great inconvenience in moving their suits by an Interpreter; they do for the most part send their children to Schools, especially to learn the English language; so as we may conceive a hope that the next generation, will in tongue and heart, and every way else, become English; so as there will be no difference or distinction, but the Irish Sea betwixt us.[26]

Unhappily, the course of Irish history has inclined rather more to the symbol used by Davies in another place, the lean cow of Egypt in Pharaoh's dream, devouring the fat of England and yet remaining as lean as it was before.

[24] Ibid., p. 153.
[25] Ibid., pp. 156 ff.
[26] Ibid., p. 160.

# Greene's Ghost in Ireland

The orygynall whye the Lord Chancellor and his brother the Bishoppe of Meathe conceyved ferst displeasure agaynste me [1]

Beholding daily with mine eyes that through the negligence of our Clergy in Ireland, Jesuits, Seminarys and fryers had free recourse not only in the country but in Dublyn itselfe, continually perverting her Ma$^{tis}$ subiects, confirming them to the pope and swearing them never to use any obedience to her Ma$^{tis}$ proceedinges, In so much that some gentlemen dutifully disposed could not rule their servants, no not their owne children, but they suddenly altered their religion & refused to come to church, to be briefe I saw that her Ma$^{tis}$ subiectes were dayly drawn to the Pope but not any one that was reclaimed in obedience to her Ma$^{ti}$. These thinges considered I delivered a booke to the Lord Deputy manifesting this & other abuses offered to her Ma$^{ti}$ through the negligence of hyr clergy. The Lord Chancellor (whom the booke did by no meanes particularly touch), knowing hys owne guiltines did not only fall into a dislike with me, but also chalenged such gentlemen of unkindnes as did but converse and hold me company. The bishop of Meathe likewise hys brother (in most unreverent manner consyderinge his place and calling) threatened me with disgraceful wordes in the open street, calling me by the name of a libeller, nothing being contained in the booke (as the Lord Deputy can testify) but that highly concerned hyr Ma$^{tis}$ service. Thus have I gotten the dyspleasure of these two prelates, the malice of whom, who is able to abide that dwelleth in Ireland, considering their authoritie which is oftener steatched out to preiudice hir Ma$^{tis}$ service then to profit it, their great combination again by the marriage of their children, for whom they provyde matches at foure or fyve yeares old, and that of the best inheritours in all parts of the country, for what is he that dares deny them but they smart for it, and more commodious it is for a man in Ireland to marry a Bishop's daughter than to do her Ma$^{ti}$ forty yeares service, and I being now disgraced amongst this whole generation, was many tymes warned of my freendes to take heed of my self, and sometimes chalenged by the Lord Chancellor's men of most shameful untruthes, intending (as I perceived) to have drawne me into quarrels the which I resolved with myself still to refuse, whereupon I came over into England, and this lent now last past, I delivered into hir Ma$^{tis}$ owne hands a small book contayning such matters as concerned hir Ma$^{tis}$ honourable profyt,

[1] Rych to the Privy Council, State Papers for Ireland, 15 July 1592.

and the bettering of hyr highnes service, the which she graciously receiving and perusing amongst other favours it pleased hyr Ma^ti that I should be hir sworne man, and I, thincking that the countenance of hir Ma^tis service had bene enough to have defended me from further quarrels, especially my offences being no other then for doing my duty to my sovereign, and comforting myselfe with this hope I presently departed back again into Ireland, but what countenance may prevaile there if the Lord Chancellor discountenance, where men dare not follow her Ma^tis service for feare of hys displeasure, where Dublyn itselfe shalbe made a shambles to murther such as shall oppose themselves for hir Ma^ti and makes those that hath great matters to deliver for hyr Ma^tis profit, that they dare not once open their lips to do it, whose mouths if they might be left open would be no small advancement to hir Ma^tis service, but, my selfe being new come over into Ireland and many surmyses coniectured what might be the contents of the booke which I delyvered to hyr Ma^ti, the Lord Chancellor who knoweth his own demeanure to be such as he dares not be without half a dozen several pardons, and being thus gauled with a guilty conscience, was easily persuaded that the book concerned hymself and his brother Meathe, and some of his owne people made me so many chalenges that it was so repeated. Imediately upon this on tuesday the 13 of June now last past, one Welche, servant to the Lord Chancellor, a Ruffyan that is accompted notorious for bad demeanure, and a common quaryler with sundry persons, and still borne out by the Lord Chancellor in manie shameful matters, as is to be proved, this same Nicholas Walshe (accompanied with sundrye persons, and brother called by the name of Peurce Walshe, a man likewyse of bad demeanure towardes hir Ma^ti, a papiste and a recusant, and yet the Lord Chancellor's man), he came unto me as I passed through the street and gevinge me most shamefull wordes, too tedyous & moste undecente to be heere rehearsed, who seeing that his rayling speeches would not prevail to draw me to that he looked for which was to quarrel, he sodaynly struck me with hys fist, and drawing his dagger stabbed at me three or foure times and withall he drew his sword, and being driven to defend my selfe I gave him a small hurt, the which hys master hearing of sent his warrant to the Sergeant-at-Arms that he should forthwith carry me to prison, and my self coming unto him to complain of his man's abuse, he called me knave and villayn, with other most unfitting names, to a man of his place, when I demanded the peace of his men he called me cowardly knave and would graunt me none, but undrestandinge by the information of others that his man had first stroke me as aforesaid, he was contented to release me from prison, and the very next day being wednesday the 14 June about 6 of clock in the evening as I was passing along the high street of Dublyn there ware six that ware layde to murther me, three layde behind a Cundytte with their swords ready drawn to do the act, and other three a little distance from them in the house of one Kelly a Surgeon, these were laid to resist if anie should offer to lay handes of the others when they had murthered me. I coming along the street passing towards my lodging accompanied by one Mr. albone Clearke, who had neither sword nor dagger about him, was not ware of this ambushe, till coming up close by the Cundytte, that all three of them starting out hewed at me with their swords, I having no leisure to draw my sword, but only with a cudgell that by chance I carried in my hand, was driven to ward and beare their blows, they driving me thus down a street before them, my foot failing me in a broken gutter, I was overthrown, and one of them, pressing hard upon me fell with me, a second striking at me when I was down. I bare his blow with my cudgill, the which being hacked and hewed before, with this blow was cut clean asunder so that I had not scarce half of it left in my hand, the third of this company likewise when I was down striking a full blow at my head, there came in a young man, whom being a stranger and who never knew me, nor I him, yet seeing me so distressed brake that blow with his sword from me, by this time I was rising on my knees, the one of them thinckinge to have run me through with his sword, there stood by a merchant of Chester called by the name of Thornton who throwing his cloak upon the thrust as it was aimed at me and by that means it mist me, being now recovered upon my feete, they yet folowed me with thrusts and blows the which it pleased god that I still bore of with the piece of the cudgel left in my hand till seeing where a door stood open I recovered a house, more then a hundred people of the city standing by and looking on, and all of them thinking that at the least I had received my death's wound, yet not anie one of them durst offer to lay hand of the partys that had offered this outrage, but they went their ways openly through the streets, towardes the Lord Chancellor's house, and the mayor of the city, who by this tyme was come to the place, by reason of the rumor, and meeting with two of them with their swords drawne in their hands, knowing to whom they did appertain, durst not demand the apprehending of them, neither would this suffice, but they still awaited me in sundry places, the very same men never shunning the towne for what they had done before, and the Lord Chancellor understanding of all what had passed would yet take no ordre in the matter, till I was enforced to fly the country for the safeguard of my life, and at my coming away was fain to be guarded aboard the ship by five or six captaines and divers other gentlemen for fear of being murthered.

Over and above its connection with the historical phase of this study, the foregoing letter has interest as offering evidence that Rych was the author of *Greenes Newes both from Heaven and Hell,* 1593.

R. B. McKerrow in his admirable edition of this pamphlet (London, 1911) ascribes it to Rych on a basis of its style and subject, and by reason of the fact that John Oxenbridge and Thomas Adams, to whom the *Newes* is entered in the Stationers' Register, had printed other books by Rych. It is pleasant to be able to add corroborative data of an external nature in support of McKerrow's view. The evidence in question is: (1) the parallel between Rych's account of the six men who lay in wait for him behind a conduit, and a reference to "knaves . . . behind a Condite" in the dedicatory epistle of *Greenes Newes;* and (2) what seems to be an allegorical fillip to Adam Loftus in the fable of the Ass and the Wolf.

The dedication is worded as follows:

To the renowned Gregory Coolle, chiefe Burgermaister of the Castle of Clonarde, Marquesse of merry conceits, and Grande Cavalier amongst Boune companions and all good fellowship; At his chaste Chamber at Dublyne in Irelande, B. R. sendeth greeting.

The prose epistle opens with an account of the author's meeting with the spirit of Robert Greene, who puts into his hands a manuscript and instructs him to see it through the press; its closing passage is:

. . . I would tel you a tale (Maister Gregory) of an Asse, who leaving the place where he was first foald, fortuned to stray into a strange Forrest, and finding the beastes of that Desart to be but simple, and had never seene the majestie of the Lyon, neyther had they felt the cruelty of the Tygar, nor had any manner of wayes beene wronged by the oppresions of the Leopard, the Beare, the Panther, or any other devouring or ravening beastes.

Thys paltry Asse, seeing their simple plainnesse, founde meanes to wrap himselfe in a Lyon's skinne, and then with proude lookes and loftie countenaunce, raunging among the Heardes, he would stretch out his filthy throate, bellowing and braying (as nature had taught him) with so hideous and horrible a noyse, that the poore beastes that were within hys hearing beganne already to tremble & shake for feare. Then he began to tyrranise, commaunding what himselfe pleased amongst them, and not contenting himselfe with that obeysance, which had beene fit for an honorable beast, and more then was due to an Asse, would many times take uppon him some duties proper to the person of the Lyon himselfe: and in the end became a notable sheepe-byter, worrying and devouring whole flockes of poore sheepe, that happened within his precincte or jurisdiction.

The Wolfe that had layne all this while close amongst the Mountaines, and having gotten understanding of the nature and disposition of this Asse, thought him a fit companion for his consortshyppe, and combyned with him in such a freendly league, that betweene them, the one taking opportunity to filtch and steale in the night, the other using his tyrany to raven and devoure in the day, the poore harmelesse Cattle that lived within their reach, were stil oppressed, & never free fro perril. The Asse grew to that greatnes that he was surnamed *Tarquinius superbus*, not that *Tarquine* that ravished Lucretia of her honour, but it was that *Tarquine* that ravished a Church of her lyvings: and an Asse I founde him, and so I will leave him.

Peradventure (Ma. *Gregory*) you expected a wiser conclusion, but what would you looke to come from a man that hath beene lately so skarred with sprites, that he hath not yet recovered the right use of his sences: it may be true that devils are afraid to passe by a crosse, but I am sure knaves are not afraide to shroude themselves behinde a Condite. You may perceive (Syr) my wits are sette a wandering, but knowing your discretion enough to conceive my meaning, I will trouble you no further, but with this abrupt conclusion will bid you hartily farewell.

Your assured freend.

B. R.

McKerrow links Gregory Coolle (Cole) with certain accusations lodged in 1588 against Sir John Perrot, then Lord Deputy, and, if we understand him rightly, seems to infer it was in this connection that Cole was sent to jail in 1592, a conclusion not wholly clear in view of the fact that Perrot was, as viceroy, succeeded by Fitzwilliam in 1588, and was himself under restraint on charges of treason in 1591. It seems at least equally likely that Cole's prudent unwillingness to give evidence against Perrot who had threatened bodily violence if he did, roused the animosity of the vindictive Adam Loftus, Perrot's bitter enemy, and thus brought poor Cole between the anvil and the hammer. There is no evidence to indicate that Cole was a member of the Rych, Legg, Pypho circle in Dublin who informed against Loftus and Meath, but the intimate tone of the epistle to *Greenes Newes* suggests a close and understanding relationship. Written as it was within two months after Rych's hasty flight from Ireland, and taken in its connection with the Loftus-Rych affair, it is no far cry to infer that the animus of the Lord Chancellor may have formed a strong common bond between author and dedicatee. So much for Gregory Cole.

Our first point, the allusion to knaves behind the conduit, needs no elaboration; concerning the second, the fable of the Ass and the Wolf, we suggest that it may be an allegorized brief of the career of Adam Loftus, he being the Ass and the "Wolfe that had layne all this while close amongst the Mountaines" referring to the Irishry of Meath with whom, as we have seen, Rych had charged Loftus with making alliance by marriage and fosterage. This would make clear such a passage as, "the one taking opportunity to filtch and steale in the night" (immemorial custom of Irish cattle thieves); "the other using his tyrany to raven and devoure in the day" (beeves being the universal Irish bribe). There is likewise an ecclesiastical nuance when the Ass becomes a notable sheep-biter "worrying and devouring whole flockes of poore sheepe, that happened within his precincte or jurisdiction."

How true to character the Ass of B. R.'s fable may have been, and who the original, remain matters for surmise, but an apter symbol than that of wolf for the wild Irish of the Tudor era would be far to seek.

# A Tudor Informer at Work

*T*HE three letters here appended, transcribed out of the Cecil Papers at Hatfield House, form a graphic record of an episode suggestive of *opera bouffe*, yet illustrative of the extremes to which the giving of "informations" might be, and was, carried in the days of the Tudors. Briefly the sequence of events seems to have been as follows:

On the third of September 1604, Captain Christopher Levens and Barnabe Rych who had served together in Ireland during the Tyrone Rebellion,[1] were sitting with a Mr. Dennis in the orchard of his house at Shanklin in the Isle of Wight. About eleven o'clock a Captain Cosnoll and Mr. Bowyer Worseley came in, and Dennis pressed them to stay to dinner. Rych, with his wife, Catherine Rych, her sister and brother-in-law, Hollis by name, Levens, Cosnoll, Worseley, Dennis, and his sister, Mistress Dennis, were all present.

After dinner as they sat at the table, someone called for the new book of statutes, and Bowyer Worseley read over the titles. As Worseley turned over the leaves, Captain Cosnoll who sat by him looked in the book, making light of the ordinances against sorcerers and bigamists. Soon the guests broke into conversational groups. Cosnoll who sat by Mistress Rych began jesting in the broad fashion of the day, and unwisely leveled one or two of his sallies at King James. When later the guests went their ways, Mistress Rych, incensed at Cosnoll's want of dutifulness, refused him the customary parting kiss.

After the guests were gone, Hollis, sitting with Rych, denounced the treasonable speeches uttered by Cosnoll at dinner. Rych hurried to his wife's chamber and finding her with her sister, the three of them patched together the conversation, Levens and Dennis confirmed it, and Rych

[1] Levens to Cecil, Cecil Papers, v. 80. 35.

wrote out a memorandum and forwarded it to Cecil. Cosnoll was in due course brought face to face with his accusers.

The Captain roundly scored Rych and Levens in Cecil's presence. He appears to have argued that the charge was brought through the malice of Mistress Rych, owing to his neglect of the customary kiss. The Rych-Levens rebuttal was that Mistress Rych had withheld the kiss out of fury at the Captain's irreverent speech against the king.

A defendant thus charged with jovial innuendo, who grounds his defense on the refusal of a kiss, is unlikely to be seriously taken even in an age as litigious as Elizabeth's. From the plaintive tone of the last letter from Rych to Cecil, we judge that Cosnoll more than held his own.

A report of certain speaches how they passed between Captain Cosnole, & Cathyryne Ryche, at M$^r$ denyses house at shanklyne in the Isle of Wight, the 3 day of sept. 1604 colected & set down by Barnaby Ryche that self & same night after they were spoken.[2]

On Monday the 2 of sept. as aforesaid, Captaine Christopher Levens & my self being with M$^r$ Denys in his orchard, between 10 & 11 of the clock in the forenoon word was brought to M$^r$ Denys that Capt$^n$ Cosnole & M$^r$ Bowyere worsely wer come to se him, who coming in made them stay to dinner, wher ther dyned with M$^r$ denys this Capt$^n$ Cosnole, bowyere worsely, Captain Levens, one John hollys, my self & 3 gentlewomen, namely myne own wife, Mrs Jane hollys her sister & wife of John hollys, & an ancient gentlewoman, sister to M$^r$ denys. Immediately after dinner, sitting stil at the table the new book of statutes of this last parliament being caled for Bowyer worsely but reading over many titles, thys Capt$^n$ Cosnoll (as it wer in a jesting maner semed by his words to make trifles of many of them viz. of that aganst sorcerers & that against the marriage of 2 wives, upon which unsemely speaches of his my wife takying exceptyons to his words they two grew into a long discourse not fully observed by any at the table, but only by Jane hollys her sister: by reason that Capt$^n$ Levens bowyer worsely & my self wer likewise reasoning of other matters, that thereby we gave no thorough heed to them nor to ther words.

[2] Rych to Cecil, Cecil Papers, v. 107. 44.

Within som half hour after, as it wer between 1 & 2 of the clock Capt[n] Cosnole & Bowyere worsely departed, M[r] denys & Capt[n] Levens going out with them where they took their horses.

The rest of the company went severall ways only my self & this john hollys remaining styll in the place wher we had dined, hollys walkynge up & down (as it wer in a petty chafe) said I se wyse men can sometimes play both the fooles & the knaves, and this he repeated 3 or 4 times together: I musing at his demeanor, asked him what thos words did mean. who answered, why did you not hear how the Captain did speak villainous words against the king: to whom did he speak those words (said I), to your own wife (answered he).

Upon thes speches I called to my remembrance that after ther had byn many words between the captain & my wife, I had hard the Captayn say that, he never before that day had hard any woman to speak so wel of the king as she had done. to which my wife answered again, that she had never yet sene the king, but she had heard al the good that she had said, & that, she had read in many books that he had ever been a godly and great & therefore she would both speak wel of him & pray for him as long as she lived.

Upon thys occasyon, calling up thes words to mind which I had almost forgotten, & remembering again that ther wer many other speches between them both, both before and after that I gave no heed unto I went to speak my wyf, whom I found in her chamber together with hir sister hollys: I asked of her what controversy it was that the Capt[n] & she had so debated on before they arose from the table.

Her answer was that she found the Capt[n] to be an evil disposed person, towards our good king, but she hoped his M[ti] should find a better affected Capt[n] when he should have need:

But yet (said I) you do not tel me what I ask you, therefore say what wer his words & how began your speeches.

To this her sister hollys answered, why did you not hear, how lewdly this Captaine behaved him self in his speaches toward the Kings Ma[ti], i lewde yenough, & I jumped Capt[n] Levens, who sat next me, with my elbow, because he might take notice of his undutiful and presumptious demeanor.

I wild them both to tel me the truth as wel what the words wer, as also how they entered into such discourse, & that they should not vary in any one point, so nigh as they could:

The matter delyvered and affirmed by them both was in this maner: that Bowyer worsely having the book of statutes & reading over the titles the Capt[n] sitting next unto him, & looking into the book as he turned the leaves, what (said he) methinks ther is an act against Jesuytes, true (said M[r] Worsely) here it is & turnyng still forward reading the titles, o (said the Captain) that acte against 2 wives & that other against sorcerers are of great importance, I promise you (which words he spake in a scoffing manner) to this my wife made another that, the statutes wer of great importance indeed, & that against 2 wives was a most godly edict, fit to be confirmed by a christian king wherein his Ma^{ti} hath expressed that vertue which I have overheard to be in him:

Gentlewoman, gentlewoman, (said the Captain, again) you have taken a good subject in hand, you may boldly speake in thys, when ther is no man dare contrary you. ther is no body can contrary me (said my wife) & I besech god to bless the king & to send him & his long to reign over us.

Well (said the Captain) the king is beholden to you, for you are the first woman that ever I heard to speak so well of the king. thes last words of the captains I remember well, my self hard him speak, & I remember in like maner my wife replied, that she had never seen the king, & that all the good that she had said she had spoken by a general report, & further more, she had read in sundry books, that he had ever been both a most gracious, & a godly king, & therefore she would both speak wel of him, & pray for him so long as she lived:

I gave no further ear to my wifes words, but she proceeded further, & said that act for the preventing of thos ungodly marriages was one of the most godly actes that was in the book.

Capt Levens, overhearing this added, & how happy are we in having such a prince, who giveth us no other laws, then thos observed by him self. he aloweth every man a wife, he craveth no more, & hath lived in all honourable loyalty even, sythe his first contract with his vertuous & royal Queen.

M^r Denys again, (as it should seem) marked those words, for he replied that his Ma^{ti} besides this continency, & sith he came into England had so demeaned him self with that honorable kindnes towardes his queen, that might give example to all married men how they should behave themselves to ther honest married wives:

to this my wife answered, marry, and he's a good king for that: but I love him as well for all other good qualityes that I hear to be in him:

I Mr^s ryche (said the Captayne) you speake thys because the king useth sometimes to kyss his wife, but ther belonges more to the matter, than a kiss.

that is truth said my wife, but what is it that the Queens Ma^{ti} hath had three or four children, besides she neither wanted dignity honor or any other pleasure that this world can afford, thankes be to god for it.

the king is a good hunter (said the Captain) & he killeth bucks, but he is good to does. and he grows weak in the back, his date is almost out!

My wife, sytting next M<sup>r</sup> denys jogged him with her elbow, that he might take notice of thes words, to the which M<sup>r</sup> denys answered, yea his date is almost out for hunting of the buck, this year, by cause they grow shortly out of season:

the Captain casting down his head said, hys back is weak, & he is going on his last half yeare:

God bless the king said my wife & I hope in god he shall live amongst us yet thes forty years.

here my wife protesteth, she was made so angry with thes words, that leaving to offend me by agravating matter against a stranger, that she had never sene before, who being a soldier, & one of mine own profession, she therefore forebore & would say no more.

having now hard the course of thes speeches, truly protested both by my wife & her sister, I immediately set them down whylst they wer fresh in memory, & then seeking out Capt<sup>n</sup> Levens, I asked him yf he had marked any part of this discourse.

his answer was that he was hartely sorry that he had not better marked it, then he did, for (said he) your wife, & her sister hath but newly delivered unto me the whole circumstance, & I remember, Mr<sup>is</sup> Hollys jogged me to several times but I thinking it was because I sat too nyre her did but verge my self to give her more room. but something I heard, something I said, but, if I had marked with consideration as I do now the maner of his speeches, he could not in such sort, have carried them away, neither do I think fit that they should be smothered. from Capt<sup>n</sup> Levens I went to M<sup>r</sup> denys, who confessed all both what hym self had said & what he heard the other speak, saying, further that the Captain was apertayning to a noble man, highly in favor with his Ma<sup>ti</sup> & whom him self did likewise honor, but as he had never sene the Captain, ner had any acquaintance of him before, so he desired no farther friendship with him whom he thought to be counterfeit papist: & therefore yll affected to the king:

other words he said unto me that I will conceal till tyme may serve, yet after all this because I would build upon a stony ground, M<sup>r</sup> denis, Captain Levens & myself being private together, I reiterated again the whole matter, that the one might witness, what the other should say, when everything again was freshly confessed, & him self rather condemned for the unreverend speeches against the prince, then hys words smothered up so presumptiously affyrmed.

Barnabe Ryche

χρofar levens

This was despatched to the "right honorable secretary ye lord cecill: principall Secretarie to his Ma<sup>ti</sup>" on 29 Sep-

tember, 1604, with a note stating the willingness of Rych
and Levens and the others named to appear and testify to
the truth of what they had reported. As a postscript we
find in Rych's hand:

We most humbly besech your ho$^r$ to perdon us in not doing this duty
our selves, who are not in case at this present to repair to your honor,
& have therefore presumed to send this messenger & the rather to help
him in the speach of your ho$^r$ we have derected his letre for the service
of the king.

The second letter, undated, and the third, dated 3 December 1604, read thus:

Most hon. Lorde, as it hath pleased you, (amongst the rest) to call
in question the matter by us informed agaynst Cosnall for the whych
we humbly thank your ho$^r$ so for the further servyce of hys Ma$^{ti}$ &
the better manyfestatyon of the trothe, may it now please your ho$^r$ to
consydre that besydes Cosnoll hymselfe ther was vii persons present
when he vented forth hys treasons, the one Bowyre Worsely hys companion at whos house is lodged (& for dyverse causes to longe here to
be expressed) that (as we thynke) wyll rather say to helpe then to
hurt hym: the other vi are all to testyfy agaynst hym: fyrst for M$^r$ denys,
he hath frely confessed two severall tymes unto us as well what Cosnoll
avouched, as to what hymselfe replyed: how he may be wrought
sythens we knowe not, for Cosnoll is a great commaundre in the I$^{le}$ of
wyght, & is ther placed in hys Ma$^{tis}$ pay: for hollys whom we knowe
to be so sylly that he is not able partyculerly to delyver the very wordes
as he hard them, yet (undre your ho$^r$ favoure) hys symply (sic) is a
good subject to boult out the truth, having neither cunning to cast
any coulers, ner other conceypt to make any florish more than is true.

For our selves, your ho$^r$ hath already heard what we have avowed, &
what we are redy further to aprove, in any maner of sort how so ever
required: for the two women, the one who especially opposed her self
to defend the honor of the king, who is fitter to deliver a truth than
she to whom the cyrcumstances of the wholl was by Cosnoll so maly-
tiously objected, but ther are exceptions taken upon a privat quarrel
about a kisse: pleaseth it your ho$^r$ advysedly to consider, she never saw
Cosnoll before that day ner since, yet at dyner time when she cam out
of her chamber to sit down, she entertained Cosnoll & worsely with
each of them a kiss. here was then no shew of quarrel yet now after
wardes yf in fyndynge hyr self dyscontented with Cosnoll for his sawcy &

traitorous demeanure towardes the king, she denyed him an other kiss for a farewell, is her testymony therefore, the worse because she hath showne her dutiful affection to her prince: for the other gentlewoman, I would it might please you ho. that the whole course of her life might be examined, yf she shall not be found to be honest, wise & of as worshypful a parentage, as any other in the Ile of Wyght, let her testimony be likewise rejected, but we hope Cosnoll can take no exception against her.

Yf all this will not serve to convyct a traitor, god save the king, & send him long to raign over us, for men shoull show more wit to pray for him in secret, then openly to detect any treason conspyred against him: we beseech your ho$^r$ to pardon our tedyousness, that do rest your ho$^r$ in all humble & dutifull affection.

χρofar levens
Barnabe Ryche [3]

To the Rt. hon. Viscount Cranborne

3 Dec. 1604

Most hon. L$^d$, for that letter brought out of the Ile of Wight by one Tho. Ore, a shoemaker, dwellyng in Bradinge, in the same isle, delivered unto us on friday this last of Nov., wherein if ther wer either forgery or falshood we know y ho$^s$ wisdom could quickly discipher, which being discovered, what had we further to say but to submit ourselves to shame & punishment, but being true as it is y$^r$ ho$^r$ may perceive how we are delt withall both ther & her, more liker of persons that had conspyred a treason then to faithful subjects, indevoring ther prince to reveal a treason: when before y$^r$ ho$^s$ face we wer so slaundred & railed at with teasynges & untruthes, but where treachery may prevayle to outbrave loyalty, it is yll for the king & worse for his true harted subjectes, that should oppose themselves in his defence, for the quarrel between Cosnoll and one of the women y ho$^r$ hath heard it is confest by all that it was after the words spoken about the king at the very tyme when he was to take his leave when she refused him, but for his traitrous demeanour to his Ma$^{ti}$.

As for worseley, a known comp$^n$ to Cosnall at whos house he is lodged in the Ile, if it would have pleased y$^r$ ho$^r$ to have marked all circumstances, he had been fitter to have been apprehended for a confederat then receved for a witnes, we are yet sure to testify for his Ma$^{ti}$. M$^r$ Dennys that is the fyft denyeth it.

We are therefore with all humblenes to beseech y$^r$ ho$^r$ to give us

[3] Rych to Cecil, Cecil Papers, v. 107. 46.

leave to appeal to the lawes of the realme, we beseech it in the way of justice, & in the behalf of his Ma^tᵗ we require it, if we shall not then by good matter as yet not heard or spoken of make manifest proof of that we have informed, we voluntarily offer our selves to death all-though the law doth not so infer against us.

Y^r ho^r as you say wil inform the king what hath been done & what M^r Denys & Worseley hath said & confest, we are likewise with all humblenes to besech you to inform the king what we have already said & what we do furthe^r protest, wherein we shall be bounde to praise y^r L^Ds justice & so long as we live to pray that god wil bles & preserve you with all honor & happines of long lyfe.

May it now please y^r ho^r to undrestand thus much further that as at first we made choice of y^r L^p in a dutiful & loving affection by us born unto you to revele this service, so now again with the like love & duty we besech that only y^r hon^r would vouchsafe us a favorable hearynge of some thing which we have yet to say & have reserved in a more honest respect than we know hath ben hytherto conveyed, which if it shall please y^r ho^r to have the hearing of, we wil then submit our selves to y^r honorable determination, you shall direct us, you shall have full authority to dispose of us, of our services, yea of our lives & all that ever we have. We rest y^r ho^rs in all humble & dutiful affection

Barnabe Ryche<br>
& χρofar levens [4]

---

[4] Rych to Cecil, Cecil Papers, v. 189. 138.

# Anothomy of Irelande

𝕿HE interesting and biting little pamphlet of "infor-mations" from which the following extract has been taken is a holograph quarto of twenty-two leaves, pre-sented to King James I in 1615 by Barnabe Rych in per-son.[1]

A fair copy, written and spaced with meticulous care, the little book is a recapitulation in form of dialogue of Irish civil and military abuses. It contains carefully worded charges of bribery and corruption against officials in high place, but not one of them is named, the object of the in-former being, apparently, to elicit definite inquiry from Whitehall.

The passage quoted in this appendix refers only to the shifts devised by Hugh Roe O'Neill, Earl of Tyrone, to train and equip his soldiers at the charge of the Crown.


The
Anothomy of Irelande

In the man^r of a dyalogue
truly dyscoverynge the state
of the cuntry

for hys Ma^tis especyall servyes
By *Barnabe Ryche* gentyllman
servant to the Kynges
most excelent Ma^ti.

[1] British Museum, Lansdowne 156. An edition of this pamphlet is now under re-vision by the present writer.

*An:* I pray *God* hys Ma<sup>tt</sup> doth not fynde it herafter, when hys houses casteles, & royaltyes, such as hath byne p served & reserved in the tyme of warres, for places of garysone, the whych houses & casteles, beynge seated in places of that Importance, that they are therfore exempted by specyall name, and provyded by acte of perlament that no *Irysheman,* shall eyther have custody or comand in any of them: but thes prohy-bytyons be so slyghtly regarded, *that some of thes houses hath byne but lately passed away, from hys Ma<sup>tt</sup> and hys heyers for ever:*

*Phy:* I thynke yt better for wayfarynge men rather to tread thos tractes allredy troden out to ther handes then to seake unknowne wayes, that yf they do not some tymes lead astray, are sure at all tymes to leade the furthest way about: and for thes presydentes left unto us by predycessours, how some euer they have byne by us carlesly neglected, wythout doubt they wer by them very provydently prescribed:

*An:* by thes neclectes the rebellyous sorte of the *Iryshe* wer made the more potent, and they wer more behouldynge to ther *Englyshe* frendes, then they wer to ther owne strenkthes ther owne wyttes, or ther owne valyance: it was they that procured *Tyrone* so many deludynge perlyes, so many *Cessatyons,* in whych delayenge tymes, the Rebelles recovered *Conaughe,* tooke *Eneskelene, Monohan,* the *Blackwater,* and supplyed them selves wyth armure, weapon, pouldre, shot, *wyne Aquavite,* & wyth all other necessaryes what so euer they wanted from all the pertes of *Irelande,* yea from *Dublyne* it self:

*Phy:* that wer strange, that so notable a traytore as Tyrone shuld be supplyed wyth any releef out of *Dublyne:*

*An:* you would thynke it strange that *Tyrone* shuld beare out the graatest perte of hys rebellyon wyth the Quens purse, and that he was supplyed wyth pouldre, shot peeces pykes, and wyth many other pro-vysyons from out of the Quens stoore:

*Phy:* that wer admyrable: and allthough thes matters be done & past, yet they be worth the speakynge of, yf it be but to gyve lyght for hys Ma<sup>tis</sup> servyce hereafter:

*An:* we have spoken a lyttel before of certeyne actes how they were ordeyned & neclected: and oure auncestors that many yeares sythens had some speculatyon into the *Iryshe* dysposytyon, foreseynge well yenough, the danger that myght insue by traynyng them uppe in any war lyke dycyplyne, for preventyon whereof they ordeyned a statute: that no *Englysh* man, that served in the cuntry wyth comand, shuld reteyne into hys company of one hundred souldyors, above thre *Iryshe* at the uttermost: but durynge the wholl season of *Tyrones* rebellyon, there wer some companyes, that for every thre of the *Englyshe,* they had thre tymes thre of the *Iryshe:* and to speake truly, it myght have byne called, a choyce & a specyal company, that had not thre *Iryshe* for one *Englyshe:*

then was ther agayne wholl companyes of the *Iryshe* that wer raysed at hys Ma<sup>tis</sup> charge: that wer as arant traytors as any wer wyth the rebelles, and out of thes companyes *Tyrone* was styll supplyed wyth souldyers, for oure Captaynes that made great gayne by entreteynynge of the *Iryshe*, that would neuer aske pay but what them selves could shyft for in the cuntry undre the countenance of beynge souldyors, would styll dyscharge ther *Englyshe* onely to enterteyne *Hors boyes* and all the rooges they could raake uppe in the cuntry, with nūbres of such as wer sent by *Tyrone* hym self & other of hys frendes: the whych beynge entreteyned, armed & trayned by our Captaynes watchynge ther opertunyte to do some exployt of vyllany, and to com yt spoyles in the cuntry wher they were ceast, thus armed & furnyshed they would rune to the reble:

*Tyrone* was thus supplyed from tyme to tyme, sometymes, wyt a thousand souldyers in one yeare all of them thus furnyshed at the Quens charges:

*Phy:* I neuer reade of any such polycy wher a rebellyous people, that wer euery day redy to revolt from ther dutyes to ther soueraygnes, shuld be admytted to the exercyse of chevallry: or shuld be Ineured in the practyse of armes: but I could set downe, a numbre of presydentes, how prudent & polytyke prynces, when they have byne so contynually vexed & molested, by such rebellyous traytors, have not onely prohybyted them from the use of weapons but have allso restreyned & depryved them from all maner of practyses aperteynynge to the warre, by the severyte of lawes

*An:* before we fell to armynge & traynynge of the *Iryshe*, uppon any ocasyon of rebellyon, a supply of one thousand souldyors out of *Englande* was thought a great matter, and all the forces of *Irelande:* durst not have incountered uppon unequall ground, but sythens we have instructed them in the knowleadge of weapons, tenne & twenty thousand have byne wyth the least for a compytent supply, sometymes in one yeare:

*Phy:* I perceyve it is oure owne oversyghtes, that have made the *Iryshe* so stronge against the prynce, & yet they do neuer want *Englysh* frendes, to perswad that ther servyce is both behovefull and necessary:

*An:* and yet thos *Englyshe* frendes what so euer they be, that doth so perswad (yf they want not wyt & Iudgment) ther honest meanynge to ther prynce may well be suspected:

*Phy:* but how could *Tyrone* be so supplyed wyth pouldre, shot, & such other necessaryes, from out the Quens stoore, as you have spoke of:

*An:* he was supplyed, by some *Iryshe* companyes that then wer in the Quens pay, that what they receyved out of the Quens store for there owne expence, they would shaare the better half wyth hym: he was supplyed by some gentyllmen of the cuntry, who undre the

pretence of makyng them selves stronge agaynst the rebelles, would
fetche from the Quens stoore, pouldre, shot, pykes armure weapon, &
what other furnyture was ther to be had, wher wyth they styll supplyed
*Tyrone* who other wyse had not byne able to have mayneteyned one
dayes feyght, but hys stoore had byne spent: then wer ther some that
would take uppon them to be *Suttelers,* to followe the *Englyshe* campe
wyth broges, wyth stockynges, wyth soope, wyth thred, and wyth such
other necessaryes fyttynge for a camp, undre whych pretences, they furnyshed *Tyrone* wyth swordes, wyth sculles wyth Aquavite, sometymes
wyth pouldre, and wyth such other thynges as he wanted, from out of
*Dublyne,* & from all other townes wher they were to be had:

*Phy:* call you thes *Suttelers,* marry they dealt but sybtylly wyth the
Quene:

*An:* some of them have dealt as subtylly wyth the kynge, that
have now but latly got so gratyous grantes from hym, as myght well
have befytted much honester men:

*Phy:* I perceyve ther is lyttell trust in the *Iryshe,* but thys makes me to
wondre, that there is not so baase a rascall in the cuntry that runes
out into rebellyon, but he wyll be followed wyth great troupes & nũbres,
comyt many spoyles, & spend the prynce great sumes of mony, before
he wyll be brought in; and it is no lesse strange, that thes baase rascales
dare ryse and rebell agaynst hys prynce, & yet daares not styre agaynst
the meanest nobleman that is in all the cuntry . . .

# Bibliography

Arber, E. (ed.), Googe, B., *Eglogs, Epytaphes and Sonettes*. London, 1563. London, 1910.

Bagwell, R., *Ireland under the Tudors*. London, 1890.

Bagwell, R., *Ireland under the Stuarts and during the Interregnum*. London, 1909.

Ball, J. T., *Irish Legislative Systems* . . . 1172–1800. London, 1889.

Bliss, Philip, *Biographical Miscellanies, being a Selection of Curious Pieces in Verse and Prose*. Oxford, 1813.
   (i) A storie translated out of the Frenche (from the first part of *Churchyardes Chippes*, 1575).
   ii) A Tragicall Discourse of the Unhappy Man's Life (from *Churchyardes Charge*, 1580).

Booker, John, *A Bloody Irish Almanack*. Waterford, 1646.

Boswell, Sir A. (ed.), *Frondes Caducae*.
  1817.
   (i) A Musical Consort of Heavenly harmonie . . . called Churchyards Charitie, 1595.
   ii) A Praise of Poetrie . . . drawn out of the Apologie, . . . sir Phillip Sidney wrote (Churchyard, 1595).
   iii) A Pleasant Discourse of Court and Wars . . . written by T. Churchyard and called his Cherrishing. 1596.
  1816.
   (i) The Mirror of Man and Manners of Men . . . by Thomas Churchyard, 1594.
   ii) A sad and solemn funeral of . . . Sir Francis Knowles. 1596.

Bryskett, L., *A Discourse of civill life: Containing the Ethike part of Morall Philosophie. . . . By Lod. Br.(yskett). . . .* 1606.

Chart, D. A., *The Story of Dublin*. London, 1907.

Churchyard, T., *A Prayre and Reporte of Maister Martyne Frobyshers Voyage to Meta Incognita*. London, 1578. (Photostat.)

Churchyard, T., *A Scourge for Rebels: wherein are many notable services, truly set out . . . touching the troubles in Ireland. . . .* London, 1584.

Churchyard, T., *The firste parte of Churchyardes Chippes, contayning twelve severall labors*. London, 1575.

Churchyard, T., *The Worthenes of Wales*. London, 1587. (Spenser Society facsimile: Manchester, 1876.)

Comyn, D. (ed. and tr.), Keatinge, G., *The History of Ireland*. London, 1902.

Corser, T., *Collectanea Anglo-Poetica, or a Bibliographical and De-*

*scriptive Catalogue of a portion of a collection of Early English Poetry, with occasional extracts and Remarks Biographical and Critical.* London, 1883.

Croker, T. C. (ed.), *Narratives illustrative of the Contests in Ireland in 1641 and 1690.* London, 1841.

*Dictionary of National Biography.* London, 1885–1912.

Falkiner, C. L., *Illustrations of Irish History.* London, 1904.

  (i)  Bodley, J., *Journey to Lecale, 1602.*

  ii)  Travels of Sir William Brereton, 1635.

  iii)  L. Gernon, *Discourse of Ireland Anno 1620.*

Gibson, E. (ed.), Camden, W., *Britannia: or a Chorographical Description of Great Britain and Ireland.* London, 1722. (Map v. II, 1327 op.)

Grosart, A. (ed.), *The . . . Prose Works . . . of Sir John Davies.* London, 1876.

Henley, P., *Spenser in Ireland.* Cork Univ. Press, 1928.

Holinshed, R., *Chronicles of England, Scotland and Ireland.* 6 v. London, 1808.

Hooker, J. (alias Vowell), *The Lyffe of Sir Peter Carewe, late of Mohonese Otrey, in the countie of Devon, Knyghte, . . . collected by John Vowell, al's Hoker of the Citie of Excester, Gent. . . . 1575.* London, 1840.

    (In Archaeologia, or Miscellaneous Tracts relating to Antiquity. Society of Antiquaries in London, v. XXVIII.)

Hope, R. C. (ed.), Googe, B., *The Popish Kingdome or reigne of Antichrist written in Latin Verse by Thomas Naogeorgus and Englyshed By Barnabe Googe. 1570.* London, 1880.

Hume, M. A. S., *The Great Lord Burghley.* New York, 1906.

Hume, M. A. S., *Treason and Plot—Struggles for Catholic supremacy in the last years of Queen Elizabeth.* London, 1901.

Hunter, J., *New Illustrations of the Life, Studies and Writings of Shakespeare.* London, 1845.

Hyde, D., *A Literary History of Ireland.* New York, 1899.

Joyce, P. W., *A History of Gaelic Ireland.* London, 1924.

Joyce, P. W., *A Social History of Ancient Ireland.* 2 v. London, 1920.

Lithgow, W., *The Totall Discourse, of the Rare Adventures, and painefull Peregrinations of long Nineteene Yeares Travailles . . .* (with cuts), 1632.

McClure, N. E., *The Letters and Epigrams of Sir John Harington.* Phila., 1930.

McKerrow, R. B. (ed.), *Greenes Newes both from Heaven and Hell . . . commended to the Presse. By B. R. . . . 1593.* London, 1911.

Morley, H. (ed.), *Ireland under Elizabeth and James I. Described by*

*Edmund Spenser, by Sir John Davies, Attorney General for Ire-
land under James the First, and by Fynes Moryson, Secretary to
the Lord Mountjoy, Lord Deputy.* London, 1890.

(i)  Spenser, E., A View of the Present State of Ireland.

ii)  Davies, Sir J., A Discovery of the True Causes why Ireland was
     never entirely subdued . . . (1612); A Letter from Sir John
     Davies . . . to Robert Earl of Salisbury, touching the state
     of Monaghan, Fermanagh, and Cavan . . . (1607); Planta-
     tion of Ulster: A letter . . . Concerning the State of Ireland.
     (1610); The Irish Parliament: Sir John Davies speech to the
     Lord Deputy . . . (1613).

iii) Moryson, F. A Description of Ireland. (Selections from the
     *Itinerary.*)

Moryson, F., *An Itinerary Containing his Ten years Travel through the
    Twelve Dominions of Germany, Bohmerland, Switzerland, Nether-
    land, Denmark, Poland, Italy, Turkey, France, England, Scotland
    and Ireland.* (1616) (rep.) Glasgow, 1907.

Munday, A., *A Advertisement and defence for Trueth against . . . the
    whispring Favorers, and Colourers of Campions.* London, 1581.

Nowell, A., and Day, W., *True Report of the Disputation . . . had in
    the Tower of London with Edmund Campion, Jesuit.* London, 1581.

O'Connor, G. B., *Elizabethan Ireland Native and English.* Sealy Buyers
    and Walker, Dublin (n.d.).

O'Donovan, J. (ed. and tr.), *Annals of the Kingdom of Ireland. By the
    Four Masters, from the Earliest Period to the year 1616.* Dublin,
    1851.

Peddie, R. A., *Printing, A Short History of the Art.* London, 1927.

Plomer, H. R., and Cross, T. P., *The Life and Correspondence of Lodo-
    wick Bryskett.* University of Chicago Press, 1927.

Public Record Office, *Calendars of State Papers, Domestic; Calendars of
    State Papers relating to Ireland.*

Rych, B., *A New Description of Ireland. Wherein is described the dispo-
    sition of the Irish whereunto they are inclined.* 1610.

Rych, B., *A short survey of Ireland . . . With a description of the
    Countrey, and the condition of the people.* 1609.

Seymour, St. J. D., *Anglo Irish Literature, 1200–1582.* London, 1929.

Simpson, Richard, *Edmund Campion, a Biography.* John Hodges, Lon-
    don, 1896.

Sisson, C. J., *Thomas Lodge and Other Elizabethans.* Cambridge, 1933.

Small, J. (ed.), *The Image of Irelande with a discoverie of Woodkarne
    . . . 1581.* Edinburgh, 1883.

Smith, T. A. (ed.), Payne, R., *A Briefe Description of Ireland made in this year 1589. . . . Unto xxv of his partners for whom he is undertaker there.* Dublin, 1841.

Ware, Sir J. (ed.), *Ancient Irish Histories. The Works of Spenser, Campion, Hanmer and Marleburrough in two volumes.* Dublin, 1809.

  (i)  Spenser, E., *View of the State of Ireland.* 1596.

  ii)  Campion, E., *A Historie of Ireland, Written in the year 1571.*

 iii)  Hanmer, M., *The Chronicle of Ireland, collected . . . In the year 1571.* Dublin, 1633.

 iv)  Marleburrough, H., *The Chronicle of Ireland, continued from the collection of Dr. Meredith Hanmer in the year 1571.* Dublin, 1663.)

# Index

Adams, Thomas, 89
*Alarm to England*, 33
*Art of Archery*, 68

Bacon, Francis, 82
Bagnal, Sir Henry, 62, 79
Bagnal, Sir Samuel, 79
Baxter, Nathaniel, 55-56
Blany, Edward, 64, 79
Blount, Charles, eighth Baron Mountjoy, 31, 50, 67, 74, 77, 80-82, 85
Bodley, Sir Josias, 3, 63-67, 70, 75, 79
*Brief Description of Ireland made in this year 1589*, 50
Bryskett, Lodowick, 41-43, 44, 45, 49, 63
Burgh, Thomas, Lord, 63, 78
Butler, Sir Edmond, 21
Butler, James, tenth Earl of Ormonde, 18, 47

Camden, William, 7
Campion, Edmund, 2, 4, 14, 15, 22, 23-25, 43
Carew, George, Baron Carew of Clopton, 74, 81
Carew, Sir Peter, 14, 15, 19-22, 28, 35, 54
Carlyle, Christopher, 42
Cary, John, third Baron Hunsdon, 31, 82
Cary, Michael, 31
Caulfeild, Tobias, first Baron Charlemont, 64, 65, 79, 80
Cecil, William, Baron Burghley, 29, 32, 33, 41, 47, 57, 58
Challoner, Sir John, 41
Chaucer, Geoffrey, 26, 45
Chichester, Arthur, Baron Chichester of Belfast, 65, 85
Churchyard, Thomas, 15, 29-32, 43, 69
*Churchyard's Charge*, 29
*Churchyard's Chips*, 29
Clarke, Albone, 88
Cole, Gregory, 89-91
Constable, Captain, 66
Cosnoll, Captain, 92-98
Cranmer, Charles, 74
Croft, Sir James, 30

Davies, Sir John, 42, 81-85
Dawtrey, Nicholas, 42
Dennis, Mr., 92-98
Derricke, John, 37, 38-41, 84
*Descriptio itineris . . . ad Lecaliam*, 64-67
Desmond, See Fitzgerald
Devereux, Robert, second Earl of Essex, 28, 48, 62-73, 74, 79, 80, 81
Devereux, Walter, first Earl of Essex, 15, 21, 28, 35
Dillon, Sir Robert, 42
*Discourse of Civil Life*, 41
*Discovery of the true causes why Ireland was never entirely subdued*, 82-85
*Discourse of Ireland Anno 1620*, 7
Drury, Sir William, 29, 36
Dudley, Robert, Earl of Leicester, 14, 29, 44
*Dumb Knight*, 69
Dymock, John, 72

*Faerie Queene*, 42
*Farewell to Military Profession*, 43
Fenton, Geoffrey, 37, 49, 79, 80
Fitzgerald, Gerald, fifteenth Earl of Desmond, 18, 35, 47
Fitzgerald, James Fitzmaurice, 18, 35, 36, 46
Fitzgerald, Sir John, 35, 47
Fitzwilliam, Sir William, 30, 33, 90
Flattisbury, Philip, 26
*Four Books of Husbandry*, 33

Gardiner, Robert, 79
Gascoigne, George, 29, 43, 69
Gernon, Luke, 7
Gilbert, Sir Humphrey, 21
Giraldus Cambrensis, 22, 26
Goode, John, 3
Googe, Barnabe, 15, 29, 32-34, 43
*Greene's News both from Heaven and Hell*, 89
Grey, Arthur, fourteenth Baron Grey de Wilton, 37, 41, 42, 44

Harington, Sir John, 63, 70-73
Hatton, Sir Christopher, 29, 43

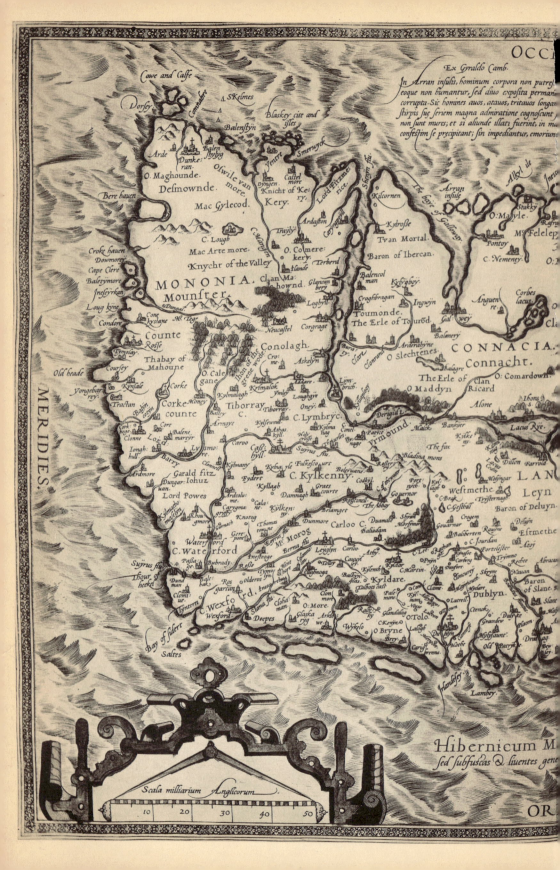